MODERN MINDS

JOSE A. RETANA

Order this book online at www.trafford.com
or email orders@trafford.com

Most Trafford titles are also available at major online book retailers.

Printed in the United States of America.

ISBN: 978-1-4907-2557-4 (sc)
ISBN: 978-1-4907-2558-1 (e)

Trafford rev. 01/20/2014

 www.trafford.com

North America & international
toll-free: 1 888 232 4444 (USA & Canada)
fax: 812 355 4082

INTRODUCTION

THE CONTENT OF THIS book has been projected to help and share with people a guide for future progress. Comparing some, old believes of the past people that tried to reach divinity thru hope and faith on higher powers of the living superior been. Reaching out eternal life; for spiritual purposes and the way to holly and pure living for all. Trying hard to find desperate ways to access the secrets of divinity and the laws involving life and death. Using the powers of the mind to penetrate in; deep the natural dimensions. To learn and understand all about the essences of living well and joyful mental states forever well, home of the living Gods.

It is also a literature for the ones coming on to be the rulers of the world once, dark and cold shadowed in the eyes of innocent and the poor because lack of knowledge and some victims of revolution cause by the disasters provoked once in a mental dimension and not recover values of mankind. It was thought for many that life was vane and care less, simple time in the land with no believes in spiritual laws; and based on brutality of the abused system on decadency cause by mental disorders in the humans that were once almost extinguish for the fury of nature. When the laws were broken and the faith, respect, believes necessary for the creation was absent from us on the planet.

1

THIS WONDERFUL TIME SATURATE with that wonderful feeling of joy so our soul be comfort and satisfy within, and ourselves every day of our precious time that we been living and the opportunely speaking generally on the planet that, we have chosen as our home and the pleasure of helping the evolution of our race already in progress. In addition, of course this day have the only meaning to live in unity of our home share by everybody in the planet because it is so interesting to belong to the kingdom of Nature; for all the time we spend in it. Now as a humans believe in our supreme and divine; of the higher power so for the honor that one can experience during the living soul and opportunity of going in the eternity with nature, our fortune of been alive is the blessings of the supreme power for me and you and so that we earned our life just the way we like to be and to preserve the privilege our stay in this wonderful world, and together helping the rest of our race and family the best way we can.

2

AND NOW; AT AGE of the boy interest in finding life more seriously and ready to affront it the best he could and, at the same time guessing in all ways and depending on him for the step next and the next for necessity and obligation of my person towards Mother Nature. In addition, along with the law governing my only life and having accepted; the pact on going to meet many adversities about to confront reality on the way of darkness and sacrifice for the reason that is hard to believe but is truth in every single part of my life. Wherever going there was something hurting at every corner of this journal doing the impossible to keep the law in my favor to be able to be in power at every time I needed to, because there was danger in it all the time and keeping my mind strong and functioning. Right during this hard time was a must in the future of the humans and nature going thru many severed changes. In addition, suffering of the elements I was force to go to where the center of activities to find the solution to all problems and causing the life in general, To be almost impossible to live in the world full of pain and suffering once, by fire and some others by extreme and horrible situations Cause by our own and brutal thinking of the victims of the tragedy; yet to come and with the desolation and disappearance of many life all over. Therefore, so during this time of darkness, I learned many things of value but the real thing is to look over us and amend the actions and reactions that come up during the interactions with each other so let us be careful of our acts before or after any confrontation with our own people, In addition do not let words or acts hurt us, in any of the many cases that can be devastating for the future later in life and work like. The one that will overcome the obstacle that was in the way of the road to infinite for there is a future for all in this wonderful and warm fire in our home. So from now on, the star will shine and shine in the high of the dark night on guide of our future and maker of our destiny and in the sky there will be a star for each one in our loving and novel planet that is our home. In addition, will be forever remembered always as our always home and living mother that as it saw us growing she like the way we talk and walk and smile. Therefore, we will see the light of sun at the east every day of our life it will happen as long as there are a children and a mother at home.

Let us this wonderful time saturate us with that wonderful feeling of joy so our soul be comfort and satisfy within and ourselves every day of our precious time that we been living as man. In addition, the opportunely speaking generally on the planet that, we have chosen as our home and the pleasure of helping the evolution of our race already exists on it. In addition, of course this day have the only meaning to live in unity of our home share by everybody in the planet because it is so interesting to belong to the kingdom of Mother Nature for all the time we spend in it. Now as a humans believe in our supreme and divine of the higher power so for the honor that one can experience during the living soul and opportunity of going in the eternity with nature, our fortune of been alive is the blessings of the supreme power for me and you. And so that we earned the our life just the way we like to be and to preserve the privilege of our stay in this wonderful world, and together helping the rest of our race and family the best way we can.

3

TODAY IS ONE VICTORIOUS day for right now life is taking the wonderful look of the very and secret form of a cloud all day long and just like I have thought she would like to celebrate one more in absolute display over the and valley where people live in union, with family and friends. And so is been a while since I was born and I keep the time closely just to see the changes of the personality for example the different on age and the different in the man's factions and especially to see how an old man looks like when is old, and the changes on the personality and, what will be the man's future in our planet. Now we keep this time to see how a man reacts in front of a situation that he may encounter, it is interesting to see that man changes according to his age and being an old man that has won the battle against time is said that we have certain number of life years and for respect because they have lived more than the young people they are supposed to know more that the young people, but this is not truth in many cases, a person well educated acts very different that other who did not have any knowledge and this is very common in today society no one knows why there are people that learned more than others and this is actually a big problem in society some people don't know much and they don't learned from others may be because they don't want to make an effort and do something on their own. But one thing is real this is because some people do have respect for others and are more careful in doing the best they can do, because that's the key to success to be as educated as one can be; so that is the treasures of the minds where all the knowledge is store and is what a person should do to learned and to work and to learned to do things on his own a job just to keep entertain and be the one he someday; he dream to be a real man with knowledge and understanding of at least the simple thing around the house, and so that this will be enough to live in today society and the prosperity will come towards the habitants of the valley and, place to try and learned what he wish to learned as a result of conscience well develop and later trained to do what he like some will do one thing and others will do something else to have the society clean strong for that, right there is the bases to prosperity and to have the real values in the conscience to and the power to be strong and useful, that is how our society will survive in modern days

4

I HAVE MANY REASONS to be thankful to God and the law of
the divine power as well as the man which is been productive
and fulfill in the earth and it is good to be alive and well in the
times where there was almost no hope for the law to impose
and to give its first step towards justice so! Now that everything
is over and done with it is the feeling is of the individual who
experience peace and justice for all because somebody gave
men, a chance to live in the name of love, and so we now live
in the places where is safe and the way is very bright and clear
to the eyes that are put in futures for good, and now everyone
will go in peace in and out the city where the operation and
reinstitution of the main group of the active and labors go every
day trying to make the best of the gift we have received from
above, and everything since to be right to the eyes opened
to beauty of nature and be one with the love and law of the
gods that create the world in an effort to make it as nice as it
can and so we now know that the life the come from above
is precious and sweet like honey and the brightness of light is

very pleasant and beautiful and all color appear in from of us as we walk towards the long lasting happiness. And now been grateful in front the eternal and powerful laws that govern our world for that we know that the truth has been unveiled and the discoveries of the leaders that take every day to the place where we can be active and see the face in the mirror and can see at the eyes, and find the peace of the creator in them will find peace in the soul for good.

And that's all there is because those who believe in god will see him in everything they see and touch because we have humble ourselves to the law and obey the gods commands in every way and everything will see and feel right as soon as we pose our eyes on it, and will find the peace in the heart already gain by the divinity and claimed by the holy spirit too;

And so welcome are the ones that where took live seriously so that they could find a place in unique and private world of love and happiness for that is fount of eternal life and precious youth as we grow in peace with the others. Because god made the whole world to live in the harmony and to enjoy it' s fruit that is the most enjoyable and precious of all gifts of Mother Nature to us we will be grateful for that always and every year when the fruit is ready there is a feeling of thanks and prayers in our heart and we pray to the lord to give us health and comfort to all of us and that we live to enjoy the fruit, product of nature and taking care by everybody that is grateful and love the garden for their fruit will keep us in wellness and forever happy in the union of lord and the eternal living; already adopted by them that has come to the world and the little ones that are promising the best of all in every way and the best wishes to them and hope to find the peace of the lord in their heart for ever in the unity of mother and father that is here to let them know all the knowledge he has accumulate during his life so that we can bring joy and happiness and pride to their parents and family in the world, teaching them how to be a good and honest individuals as they will want to be and find the fountain that never stop running down the mountain every day and every night like a wish he made to the gods he would like to have as your and so for their well been in general make the best of their life, and so that is why tonight we must be very proud of them all.

5

THE TRIUMPH TO OVERCOME the obstacles on the way to divinity and happiness and abundance on the earth life and the journey to infinite already prepared for any adversity in long and dark journey towards the realization of the changing world ahead of us. Having to deal with the natural laws secret and powerful as the universe; when it comes together as one; far from the destine. I travel thru long distances dark and remote where no one has gone. In addition, we come already prepare too many adversities encounter in life sometimes difficult to understand, but realities that come from our minds personalizing; Our conscience really identifies the humans that are in the time of obstacles to the realizations of the individual's life. Impedance of life, these are dark spout in the mind of the individuals who cannot reach the top of the mountains; Many are called by not all will make it, for the reason of training and capacities in our minds. In addition, the abilities that are missing in our life because of no interest in better us, In addition, reach the states of mind required in life to live in peace with others. And to be able to produce for ourselves are recommended to each and every one interested in the realization of our minds; with purposed of caring himself to divinity. Now time has told us the mysteries of life and we have witness the past as example of field across and the devastation of humans that were victims of a very bad and dangerous state. When seen the tears and cried that came on when Jesus was found in the planet and came down to bring a message to everyone. So we can be save from the devastation that left many marks in the mind trying to get out of the horrible state in which we were not knowing, the real cause of the suffering and devastation. In addition, the planet but now we all come to reality we come to encounter the real meaning of our life and the reason to be with the law of God. In addition, to be holly and secrete and to become one more or; will work and care for each other and bring the message to the children in earth and to go on to divinity and have eternity to. Enjoy the most wonder and colorful pastures to where one can live in harmony and no one can take away the treasures of the mind.

6

HI TONIGHT THERE IS something In, that has us keep in suspense and it is because the actions we take in favor or against ourselves or o our own person that concerns you and me and the other humans we lived for so long in the planet. And so now I want to do something to correct this errors cause by men and of course concerns all of us deeply in our spirit and physically sometimes wounded and deeply hurt by others that not only think low and no sense what so ever, and so! We see incidents on different kinds of humans with clear differences in opinion and actions taking by these too. This is been going on for a long, long time and it's the root of the misery and poor usage of our mental abilities giving to us since we were born. Now it comes to my mind that we, man has been wrong about each other mentally and physically aggravated for the simple reason that we have not been correct ourselves from those identities growing in the internal world that concerns the spirit in us and it is real that we all have been provoked and seriously hurt by some other human been, at these point it is important to realize that when there is a problem and it cause obstacles on the way that conduces to the everlasting life as every man always dream of in our existence in the planet. And so we experienced many things! like love like hate, or other some good and some hazardous to the delicated been inside and it is for that reason we are not permit to keep our human figure no longer because the fact a man should be peaceful and not violent as the history has thought us in the past, something very wrong happen in the creation along the way, where we were assaulted by the forces of our own nature and we were transformed into the dirties race over the planet and for this reason a catastrophe was about to destroy man who was involved as the most recent and intelligent been ever created by nature and gone to! be the most unfortunate individual of all, and so that is why we are here today fitting for our life and trying to make a better way to live since the second coming of Christ and for that reason now the judgment day has come for all for nothing has changed and no one put interest in better themselves because the fact that man at this time had no believes in and no respect for one another, and so the time is coming now when we have to go on our own destiny for that was what we made of ourselves ever since.

7

IN A LAND WHERE no one goes, and the wild smell makes itself notice as I approach the remote land and the sound of the leaves make by rain thunder and lightning! Sound like something never hear by me, and because the tenderness the road that conduces to these land was so beautiful I pray during all the journey while every once in while reach in my packet to get some precious candy to eat and pass the time away in the way to the land of rain. In addition, because of it exotics plants grew at the side of the road and the birds sound very mysterious to me somewhat sad many times! Then as I, traveling steel far from my destination and my body got as exhausted as I could and in addition the sunlight was despairing! That's when I figure there trouble was just starting, it may be my imagination I thought to myself; as we enter into the shadow and deep in the forest and the rain do not seen to stop may be that would wash away the terror and the tears with its gentile touch over the face, and so the intrigue come to be very bad, like if something very bad was already happening so! A short while later the cloud of the rain make me shake hard and my teeth sound too and the eyes were too wet to try to see any more, but I have to somehow go even farther into the jungle suddenly it happened again everything turned into total darkness like if there were no more life ahead of me, hopefully if stand and try to go and find the trail that would get the next house and my eyes were again restore to see where I was... at same time the rain wouldn't stop and more rain steel to come and the river that runs thru these valley do not stop grounding the rocks in it, sounding like the sound of death from beyond where no one knows what's after it

8

THIS DAY HAS BEEN pleasant and joyful to all because no one suffers any more from lays and false prophets and there were numerous everywhere they could be and for the same reason problems came to us falling into ignorance and the false statements that make us victims, with no arm to defend and fight for our life so many times falling in the deep sleep like with a wondering mind with no realism at all. But since it was so, a man with authority and educated, with the truth in his verb sincerely try to teaching the secrets hiring of nature, to the people just trying to protect them from ignorance and chaos in the peoples life, some did not put attention require to practice his teaching and ideas to end the problems of the population then, with the knowledge to unveil sincerely, uncovering the teachings and the secrets of heaven and beyond. The expender and vocation makes us sane and happy, on the meetings he was seen in different places showing the evidences to us and making us his friends and family giving life to everything he touch along his trail in whom we believe as the savior and leader of the world and they saw and attend against while some believe and will enjoy his verb and the miracles and wonders it would bring, rushing and calling to the awaking of the new era and the revolution of the incognitos writings and teachings seen in all times recognize and arms against evil in an effort to bring conscience to waking at new world and all people the wants to learned and live according to the law of the gods and bring peace and prosperity to these land and study interesting them of present and past walking fast toward the new era awaking us at the discovering and advances of the world. Humbly serving the knowledge to approach all kinds of human of the world to bring them everlasting life and more join them to feast of the universe and abundance and many fruit to eat for all since it's the feast of the hearts to the lord and we offer Him our prayers and hymns and sacrifice and to labor the field to make us humble and servants to be free

9

ONE MORE OF THE students of exoteric and occult knowledge of the Gnostic movement, as we go along in our life we find more them that can be study and help us enrich our life, for that reason is that we are launching at this moment that Gnostic knowledge to anyone who likes to make his life rich and pleasant, and I have to make mention about the functions of our system centers like mind, sex, and spirit that together make a man an important figure of the universe and to keep our life there are some things we must do because since his appearance in the planets it has make a big difference in life in general because the world turn to be very different as it was planned for everybody at the moment, and so since the history of man there has been thoughts in the rise, both good and bad and so and since man it's a combine elements in one and since it has become a power of his own no longer can take the position nature's laws and forces as one with nature, but it becomes something more in its conditions of living with the rest of life and it's for that reason that we have been called to be rulers of the nature's laws and then the choices of becoming part of it and be an individual power that will make a difference in life in general has become number one issue at these time, because for some reason man thought to be wrongly the immoral and indestructible been in the planet, but now we all know that it's a little more complex than we thought because of the reason that we have abandoned nature's principles of living like the love and care, and also dedication of our life and be the figure as the rulers of the world has been in decadence since man the fall that took place in the mind of been the figure that will give the example to all of us and to guide the rest of the people thru life so that everyone would be super-figure of the universe and the fault made by the this figure on is presence in our world became in danger of the life and the loss of his powers and even further much more the suffering of the individual at the mercy of his own sins. And my life is full of choices, in order to become perfect at some point we make another decision and the consequences of the repeatedly make the same mistake is the sin and to interfere in this manner is to become sinner and produce the loose of the powers in general until it comes to be what is called death. The process of this phenomenon is very tragic in the individual because the mind will disable and to lose the body is inevitable. Now the unknown has become interesting knowledge for those interested in discovering the mysteries of life. For this is our goal and presence in this planet, not to live in discordance with the other because life is the living and thinking eternally is for us the recompense of the work we do in the planet and from above our heavenly father is looking as we are called nature's son, because is of course where we all come from, and as we develop our mind and recognize the law, everything will be as we planned for the reason that life is our gift from above, and we received the confirmation and resurrection every single day of our life and living for the cause in our minds to live in the world of happiness plenitude because life is inner thoughts of our been internally and humbly working towards the perfection of the laws and mechanisms to fall in place one and every time we are present on the face of the planet

10

LET US NOW TALK about our interesting them of the loving, to start we can say that is interesting and beautiful topic that I think we have in the past underestimated and missed use in many ways that everybody have to put the most attention as we could because is true the alarming use of the reproductive system as an important part of the human been that already in an alarming percentage have committed during our life and so that why we want to talk about in this session of our dedicated studies and now rushing it would be nice to address closely and delicate I must say for the reason that this center is the delicate site in our body that in charge of the procreation and it's delicate and tender tissues that once destroyed is in general very hard to restore because is our life itself what we deal with at the present time; as we compare it as a little tree that grows in fresh soil and tenderly develops itself in an effort to give life one day on its own but at the begin only the love that god puts in it will make it grow to be a big and strong tree. Like we already mention he has to be taking care of by others or be in the right place to grow all in his own, taking advantage of the natural rain and light from the precious atmosphere, that in the case it grows by itself and with the help of the love mother nature can give him every day and by the night its roots growing inside the pure soil where it was planted or where it was born by the grace of god. By now we all know the secret of love and the creation of nature in the wild country where we were born and then the time was develop to as a mark of god to related to his been since he was born and his body was develop to from the very soil, from mother nature one more of the love which grows and grows in it spirit to so as we see the spiritual side of nature is so important in life and grow in the spirit of the body that we all own; as the temple of the living soul and future father of the little ones to come and of tender love is necessary to grow in harmony in this call! Life And so to have a son or having a one is like it's been sad it's born in the moments of a conception and that, comes from mutual love sharing and working on- together with the fire and the seminal substances representing the water that makes the tree grow to be and making it what it will be in the near future, based on that we can say... Life develops and evolves inside the nature's big laboratory always working with our natural elements that live in nature; living and in it because is life is the potential of a living creature coming from the deepest of the forest of our nature potential to be a man or any other creature in our kingdom to represent the spirit invisible to the eye but detected by the faith, believe in the higher power only the individual knows if is life and what we represent in our life. You could say that life will never stop processing live internally, in the deep and we the ones the comes from latest creations to be able to do any good changes in nature's structure, call to after many changes be a world ruler so much that everything obeys to him because He loves and cares for every other one making life easier every time for his especial functions and gray powers, been created to be nature's guide, coming from fire and water as the elements that power the world and its reproduction which is life and the miracle of reproduction or the miracle of life perpetual

11

ACCORDING TO THE WORLD of god and the law in life is applicable to every living been in our universe, for us to be save and to be an active and humble man that can be trusted by the honor of the world of his own + to make the verb of the soul in the unity of the body and the spirit, and make the most of what he spoke in worlds and to make materialize his verb and to be reality of the world for the sound of the voice is hear in every corner of the world and beyond the limits and frontiers because him one he say to do what he wanted to say in front of the gods an all the ones that represent the law and they always make the law take place every time in the name of the lord who live and rein in the high of our souls that speaks with the truth always because, of the power of the verb it so! Secret and powerful for making the god's will and the music the universe was hear all over, the pleasure of speaking the visions of the mind and to hear the ocean in the profound and mysteries of it, is like a tale of an unknown and dark place for a children in a conversation with the granddad because he was fascinated about the voice of the ocean, but or a man to go into heaven is more complex and courageous than it looks at the first impression and it comes from the deepest of soul where resides and the heart is his develops and goes out as a symbol of the sound the heart makes something describe in the worlds of the been, so that we can understand the kind and the origins of the a man when he or she wants to express his feelings or to describe the ideas of the mind on the wonderful sense of the speech, very important for the relations of man and nature too.

And so from the time we were born and the power of the speech was growing and developing the kid sad little and when learning the use of the senses like vision, voice, smell, hearing and testing the babies grow slow so he can learn all the abilities of his soul and body for later use and to become a real man. Practicing these powers is very important to us for later use in life, And following the line of the child when it becomes a man in a direct experience I remember this process to be very interesting since is a way of learning to use his powers and, also the mind become more active and stronger.

12

ONCE THE RAIN CEASED, the country start to fall in the deepest and profound dream of warms and because the soil was wet and mud from the saturated soil from where he summer flowers would come and also the dry dust save the fallen seeds for later in the next rains will make nature fertile and exotic forever. So we all come out to give the welcome to this summer because like every kid likes; is to play in the outdoors with the things founded and gather ready to play outside the house, when the sun shining in the height in the middle of sky to stay in and for the summer hoping it stayed for a long time so we can play with friends on town. So now is the middle of the season and everyone has projects to do and as school start the students go in the morning and come back for the afternoon joyful and grateful with their mom that send them to study every day and the weekend will be dedicated to Sunday school in post of knowledge and devotion about god and the forgiveness of our sins in case the divine law was broken and the salvation of our soul from evil and the mistakes committed against god law and to give only sacrifice to mother nature for been so kind and put some food on our house so we don't suffer from hanger and for keeping the family aware of the need to make our sacrifice to our brothers and sisters in needed help. And one day when no one was around and the silence was his only companion making the effort to take your steps stood up and walk in his own and to be in the way to man of love and love because he decide to make the world better and save and to gather the material to prove one day in the teachings of Sunday school and the principles of a well form and productive life in the way to success and to make a family of well been to make the dreams of the gods at night looking down from the stars joyful and proud to be alive and well that's he dreams and from there, Life was an open book full of wonder and miracles in the way to be the man one day took refuge in the sides of the road and on to gather proof and evidences to say that life can be more than a passing time in the planet empty and full of our own dirt and soul of a monster waking in to the way where no one is saved and to give up life for the pleasure of committing sin. And to revel against god laws which gave us the true and wonderful life of a wonder inside deep in the soul for the good lord protect us from and deliver us the untrue and cruel tool transformed into weapon just to satisfies the evil mind with no other thought in mind to stop the brother and keeping him from been blessed by the law. And so since then this little man obey the law and will sacrifice for the ones in need and thirsty for a drink of water in a summer full of wonders and life to live it...

13

ON THESE DAY WE have come with the purpose of continue studying in which may be fascinated and important too; including the elements of life over of the so perfect unlimited universe imaginary we stand on the middle of it. As for enchant the universe is beautiful and invite us to enter on the most unknown places ever touch by a human. The creation and its activities that keep us in order and in movement until dark when we rest and. Where talking to ourselves we find many answers to what are at times mysteries of the mind and at sunrise, what a surprise of the things going thru the sleeping mind and body as the night comes into town and the shadow makes everybody to go and dream to the next day exactly at rise. So early in the morning when it fresh and dump taking a step outside the house to breathe the air charged with hydrogen and all the elements combine like if it was a new life just began for all. And so it is us to study and get knowledge at the reach of our friends and family to enjoy and to enrich the minds and to share the spiritual side of nature with is best to and flowing thru and out of the mind making the verb in the mouth preciously pronounce for the ones the knows these knowledge. Because they work on to tell their grandsons from mouth to ears the experience lived for prophets throughout the world. As the privilege to belong to the world and to live in divinity and knowledge as the chosen ones directing destinies our future and a silence on our heart and the universe for the spirit and experience much bigger than it was before. In addition, even Mother Nature enjoys because love is for all, going in to divinity and just of the law of god will remain with us.

14

I HAVE TODAY THE opportunity of living in the wonders and changing dimensions of the universe, because god our farther and guide have me and you in the presence of the universal of unbreakable and defined merciful laws that governed us as one, in the unity and of our father. And for the most wonderful reason of the beginning of the new era of the changing and developing universe, so we all together we shall give him thanks and prayers so that we can see the new world and it's wonderful creations, in this case and for the sake of our sons so them to have the opportunity of see it and inherit the delicious and colorful rims of life in union and the security of the community as one.

When everything start and the world began there was glory and there was hope that one day the wonders and powers of the lord would come upon us to make us love and happiness for all of us and the day for to come to live in unity of the holly spirit of our lord god and father of the universe in a changing and developing of the creation and the rising of the human races all over the planet according to the prophesies of the past and the

27

future to, for that idea and the opportunity giving to us as a gift from above, for every one alive and willing to be a man of the truth and love for the plan god had for us.

So let me say that after seen the wonders of the universe I ask myself what will be in the agenda to make the races and all others been realize the importance of the work upon ourselves and the promises of our lord from above to make us humble and to make us god's living souls that opportunely bring us to live in a place of harmony and richness for all to help and to give the sons the opportunity to be one day our changing world.

15

Our destiny. Man has risen and today more than ever, we have come to see the future of the entire and majesty of a perfect world. And just before our eyes he has put the picture and our destiny and the future of the race. For the people who believe in the supreme power and had the faith and the devotion for the power of the lord as the guide and truth that he spoke, thru the choose to accomplish the mission and the encuentro with the law and came across the land and overseas to see the changing world and to be able to steal learned with each other in order to become masters in every profession and every event that man could imagine and in order to take the truth to all people living on the planet and to encounter the force that put the human mind in danger and to save the ones one day came to the world to simple have a time for themselves and to know the real life as a man and to enjoy the fruit of the gardens all over the planet, and so here I believe we encounter each other and we were full of joy for our little brothers and little sons in our life as a man, so when the time is in our favor and we think in every one and I see their face and the smile in your face I don't see nothing but pride and joy for you because everyone that are in the planet has come down to earth to participate in the rites of nature and to come to be with our brothers and our sisters in the planet and for the reason that we can cooperate with each other In an effort to overcome the forces of nature and to make a safe place to live and to encounter the future of the world to come and to learned the different ways of living in the planet also to encounter our laws and to preserve life at its best and also become a more stable and more sophisticated ways of living.

16

AND ONE MORE OF the most individuals that have many interests in the occult knowledge of principles, obligations of our most secrete moments of our life for all created, by this nature in evolution; based on what we call love, understanding, and much work in our nature since the appearing of man, which cause an impact of the most cruel and the most unfortunate of all been so as we come down and realize the future of the race of humans that appear in and during the evolution of all life in the planet, at this point all nature saw the tragedy of the human life that took place in the planet long ago, and the unfortunate figure of the race when we were still part of nature, but at the same time it was mostly because the wrong doing in our part, and no good living indicatives of sanity and common sense and soon after we were born this been confront the deadly and most unfortunate situations in their life according of what happened in our not too long ago past that took place in this planet. Now we can all have some understanding of our past as our ancestors could not make their way thru and perishing in hell for most our time when we were only an idea of man, and now we must, must understand the importance of living according to the secrete law that we have to obey and enforce this commands to go and make our way thru living with honor and to defend and protect our family against any force that may harmed and make an obstacles in front the way causing the fall of any of us and to be ashamed of, and correct it the wrong doing since man's fall long ago and since then we been looking for the cause and solutions to the problem of suffering and death of the falling civilization of the empires of the world. And now that we are all in our state of the sanity giving away from the law and its most closed sources of giving life that is our nature's laws according to the faith of every different one with and for all the goodness from the higher power to protect and defend the ones that has at least the willpower to repent and to amend the sins created during the time in the planet. For that and for more I say that all the sins has been forgiving and washed away with water of the fountain of youth that comes down the heist mountain in the place we live and so for that we give thanks graces to the lord for been so loving and kind to forgive us and deliver us from evil and protect us from the cruelty of evil and dirty and instead give us strength and keeping us from falling the hands of death and to keep us healthy to confront the adversities of things that are impossible of change and to welcome the things that are good for us and the family that stud together in the adversity of life and in the good time that we could share in life too for because made us strong to fight the evil and to be in peace with the law forever.

17

EVER SINCE I WAS born and soon after I was capable of walking; my mind develop quickly because In part I need to take charge of things; first around the house and soon I realize that the urgent need to learned as much as possible first because the world was at the time of my birth very wild and at time very cruel and incomprehensible hard to understand because no one seen to be capable of seen the reality and the importance of taking life as seriously and no one seen to care much about for some specifically not known to humans at this time, which they were incapable of seen reality and denned life's purpose at this time, for reasons of mental and physical information; for we lived in false and in denned state of our own life. Provably because of the way we turned to be later after our appearance as a living independent and auto-power and supreme been, and no longer capable of controlling the very strong and incontrollable thoughts, later victims of the pain and suffering, steel not in control of himself, for the reason of the unknown and dangerous state of mind at that time. And so this is what was happing when I came on and saw all happening right in form of us and my mother told me to be award of the we do so we do not get In trouble and go to the school just like ever body else to learned something and to meet people in the growing town were our school was some miles away from the house. Since I didn't understand all the situations that were going on I decide to take one at a time and pass unnoticed during the time was there and more. Little by little everything stared to change but that doesn't mean that it was going to be easy instead life was thought and we started to lose hope in the middle of all world looking and watch by at all time. And so one of this days a suddenly the ideas became more clear and my vision was even more clear to open my eyes and see the real me inside and out and I made the decision of going ahead with the plans we already made long, long ago and to coupe with agreement made by us in desperate times when we were able to see each other now if we now can say that one day god will keep us in mind so that can have the peace in our spirit and some comfort In our body for this is what we all need long ago. Thinking in a reasonable manner I am center and no longer have fears for my well been because it can be at times very hard to coupe with problems in the mind on physically hurt that a man can sooner or later die from those controversies and no longer function and now for the grace of god life is come back to many of us and so much more like this young boy that didn't have a chance with the society doing so bad, it was hard to see reality, because the past societies did not put order and no one had the chance to learned something useful like if there is a soon time.

18

IT IS TIME TO come forward today and be the One! That has a life on to be the one! The only that can take the road ahead with only one purpose, to live on the stream and the path of life in yourself, taking blame for the acts one has been doing, and so when it comes to work on one's internal world going inside the conscience and looking at the window of the past it comes to us what you are in the real life is the one in the present too and you in front of yourself to see the values granted individually for you, so we can say that when it comes to work on better yourself and do something that has values on your favor it is like having currency in hand to utilized in your favor when needed this process is call karma and goes in your favor helping the individual progress without having to stop your thinking flow that will permit him to win the case against the obstacle in front of you and consequently leaving the rod clear incessantly so we can follow the this current and constant flow of life, and so having said this we stand by strong so nothing can stop any of us and like other has, will educate himself in the eternal lake of life in company of the family, providing the support necessary to be the one that one day was small and innocent but thanks to the effort and courage and the treasure he has since the beginning of his life they took advantage and put in practice the knowledge from above sending the energy and taking the law in and as a defense he work on the developing of our life and reinforcing nature laws by working internally and constantly with the law in direct access this the universe for the good and to put the rest of us in a good position fighting for the most novel purpose, !getting them out of the stage of unconscious and the deepest sleep of us since one can remember, so now that we can with the knowledge in hand ready to use as somebody use a weapon with tremendous power on his hands, so when are we going to be responsibility of the life we have inside our bookies call spirit from above taking care of this and realizing the magnitude of the problem that we have against ourselves in order to live so that we can go and humbly ask for the fogginess' of our sins and grateful ask for help from the lord to keep our life vigilantly and safe so for that we give thanks pray so that it can be done in the father that reins and governed our system.

Much too learned from Mother Nature and ourselves and we did not do it.

19

AT TIME COME FORWARD today and be the One! That has a life on to be the one! The only that can take the ahead with only one purpose, to live on the stream and the path of life in yourself, the acts one has been doing, and so when it comes to work on one's internal world going inside the conscience and looking at the window of the past it comes to us what you are in the real life is the one in the present too and you in front of yourself to see the values granted individually for you, so we can say that when it comes to work on better yourself and do something that has values on you it is like having currency in hand to utilized when needed this process is call karma and goes in your favor helping the individual progress without having to stop your flow that will permit him to win the case against the obstacle in front of you and consequently leaving the rod clear incessantly so we can follow the this current and constant flow of life, and so having said this we stand by strong so nothing can stop any other has, will educate himself in the eternal lake of life in company, providing the support necessary to be the one that one day was small and innocent but thanks to the effort and courage and the beginning of his life they took advantage and put in practice the knowledge, from above sending the energy and taking the law in and as a defense he work on the developing of our life and reinforcing nature laws by working internally and constant law in direct access this the universe; for the good and to put the rest of us in a good position fighting for the most novel purpose, !getting them out of the stage of unconscious and the deepest sleep of us since one can remember, so now that we can with the knowledge in hand ready to use as somebody use a weapon with tremendous power on his hands, so when are we going to be responsibility of the life we have call spirit from above taking care of this and realizing the magnitude of the problem that we have against ourselves in order to live so that we can go and humbly ask for the fogginess' of our sins and grateful ask for help from the lord to keep our life vigilantly and safe so for that we give thanks pray so that it can be done in the father that reins.

20

JUST LIKE ANY DAY they will come and go but today a special one for life an time, because it never stops and so it is a mystery to us how it happens, day after day we carry away these force of nature and it is true these happens day after day noticing our life in lengths of time of days months and end of the years managing our life with these force call time that will track everything alive going around our life as the clock marches every second as unknown mystery of nature and the humans are exposed to these phenomenon like all others in the planet since the birth of the individual been lights at the day of his birth and from there man cause many other life to rise as a product of evolution and power to The will power of man and nature, as one in harmony and mutual collaboration. But as we live on to eternity and the field of life of the individual must go along with very little help because it is up to the One, the individual who will raise towards the future the only one the will make the decision for him as a especial specie that was born from nature most powerful refined evolution in our life. Figuring out the gift of life and be successful when going across the field of life, finding out wonders in the mind and realizing the obligation I have on myself and other life around us and to contribute to the rest with goods manners that accept and please nature knowing that no one else life if you don't want to for the reason that I have to live by and for the law and live every day in peace with the rest and most important of all with ourselves on the care of our God as guide and support and life is nice to live with peace and love in the unity of the internal conscience and soul possess by only one person the inner been as the life that was giving to us in the begin and hopefully perpetually of time to live in time possess by our soul and human spirit to stay in this world and to recognize that we come from nature and steel are in nature for eternity and in unity of the all that come along with us.

21

TENDER MINDS AND AGES that a human been has to confront in the early days of his life, when just! A life begins. Kids or baby animals has to learned the tasks necessary to be a successful member of the family and especially be responsible for his or her own learning process because, suppose that a lion in his early stage do not show any learning skills and then he will be unaccepted to the rest as they have hunt for survive and be able to take care of himself but if he learned and provides. Not only for him but also to his own need he becomes useful for all as a group therefore, he can be a leader. A good leader will direct for as long as he lives. And so when it concerns man or mayor authority animals is truth that we tent to behave uncivilized for lack of principals gather in the early days of our life or in other words no good values that can governed in our minds and so, the lower and uncivilized. Behavior domain the in our minds causing problems in our conscience and physical illness that cause our death and suffering Contrary to that we see that some people get along one hundred per cent. Which other support, love, and that makes the group very strong keeping the family, as known in most cases to groups that live together for life. So man is known for living social for that reason society has rules like all the groups in every kingdom that we know including us, because nature acts very similar in all we are supposed to belong to; a universal group sharing the space every day. Therefore, for that we are up to live and get along because of that we have to obey the laws that apply the individual in the place and in the minds, the spirit! To comply to with our responsibility with each other and especial to be always in grace with nature for the opportunity of becoming part and independently as well, for life become communal. We want to become the survivor ones, because if someone do not live in the community and the community; is something that acts in favor of all that love one another. That is why communities are strong and loving to each other for love is very important in life of the community and necessary to man. In addition, this one fallows rules to assure the stability of our benefits and the spirit at the very best, because love is big and strong in the life. Every community and joyful town in growing and beautiful meetings that everyone enjoys from time to time in town to even more making it super rich in every way we can.

22

THE EVOLUTION OF MAN; man must evolution equal as nature does it is learning too, because that; what it means evolution is to overcome the laws of the wild and therefore to stay alive when one thinks and feels comfortable in the state of mind that we choose. In addition, to become psychology active so that the mind body and soul be permanently alive, cause by its own evolution If the individual is ready. Evolution is a law too and so we all must comply with this and the other laws. Because of this laws that we must comply, we earned life as you like to be, now a mind that progresses in evolution it means that is learning and it is gaining experience and he take absolute control and care of himself. A good example is a child born learns to eat, walk reads works etc., and then he or she will be ready for eternal or temporary life. Meaning that you are aware of yourself one hundred per cent of what you are and what you want to be in the future. Accepting other things to be around and to love one another is part of been a human that wants to stay in his state. Because if people do not accept each other is a state at fault and must be overcome somehow

The learning state of the mind it is like a physical training for and event as the Olympic Games it helps to select the best ways of going ahead. Actually man state of mind is critical and it needs the evolution so that man overcomes the states that impedance man to keep ahead learning the facts of life, and to think and our own future as a way to keep evolution to reach eternity, cultivating and working with the row materials to keep alive and well. In addition, mature enough in the centers that constitutes a human been, sexually mentally and physically capable of going beyond the present and into the future Time is our learning director capable of desiring the number of years allowed or assign to our life. In addition, man responsible to take serious the purpose of life to be successful, in our evolution path.

23

THE TIME WHEN WE all meet together and hold hands in glory and power of the living god and be the ones that has the victory in the internal fire as we all come a long way since the start of life, and the beginning of life as we go thru and in to the beyond where the forces and the powers of triumphantly will humble will congratulate each other in a sign of peace and intelligent that one day went to and in search of his life in a world full of danger and crimes that will affect the centers 23

The time when we all meet together and hold hands in glory and power of the living god and be the ones that has the victory in the internal fire as we all come a long way since the start of life, and the beginning of life as we go thru and in to the beyond where the forces and the powers of triumphantly will humble will congratulate each other in a sign of peace and intelligent that one day went to and in search of his life in a world full of danger and crimes that will affect the centers in the inner of the soul and the beauty of the body radiantly with, as fire of the night, and the movement of it surprised everyone in the planet. Many years past and we steel are possess by the feelings and the terror of the war which to place inside our own place where we live and go to reunite in secret when we are already has overcome the forces against the survival of the one called masters of the philosophy and the persecutors of the crime of the so called negative values of the human been, and to be able to develop many of the values one need to survive as a man active and intelligent enough so he can be a self and more sufficient individual with future on his hand control and regulated by himself with many positive characteristics necessary to take any individual thru life and his secure home to live in because that precious and wonderful values inside making him strong and flexible minded personality to battle the forces of evil that are nothing but the one in the side of the darkness inside you that make man what it is today and with prove of what's done inside the conscience about the work over one and concisely worked on by him in the struggle for survival as part of the evolution and the willpower for the man's verb takes place in active and strong presence of the world the people who one day dedicated their life to prove reality in front of everyone. Therefore, capable of mining his world of honor and in the name of the law creates a wonderful society down in the planet and beyond.

In the inner of the soul and the beauty of the body radiantly with, as fire of the night, and the movement of it surprised everyone in the planet. Many years past and we steel are possess by the feelings and the terror of the war which to place inside our own place where we live and go to reunite in secret when we are already has overcome the forces against the survival of the one called masters of the philosophy and the persecutors of the crime of the so called negative values of the human been, and to be able to develop many of the values one need to survive as a man active and intelligent enough so he can be a self and more sufficient individual with future on his hand control and regulated by himself with many positive characteristics necessary to take any individual thru life and his secure home to live in because that precious and wonderful values inside making him strong and flexible minded personality to battle the forces of evil that are nothing but the one in the side of the darkness inside you that make man what it is today and with prove of what's done inside the conscience about the work over one and concisely worked on by him in the struggle for survival as part of the evolution and the willpower for the man's verb takes place in active and strong presence of the world the people who one day dedicated their life to prove reality in front of everyone. Therefore, capable of mining his world of honor and in the name of the law creates a wonderful society down in the planet and beyond.

24

IN THIS OCCASION WE like to take the opportunity to mention some important themes that affect our life directly, for some reason we think that life is, something to temporarily, and meaningless and with careless and moral values, because there is no one to go affront, and make an explanation of the acts, and its final results, of the acts towards another person or any other form of life, and taking careless of what happens we act irresponsible and cruelty, because one does not have the appropriate steps and take the responsibility of this crimes, we have to be alert for the people who commit the crimes towards other people or other form of life, including elemental life, and so every day there is something done against nature form the men figure that keep acting against other without any sanctions; because this individual are hopeless and disable to do anything since long ago because the fact that in the eyes of the law the necessary steps has to take place in the appropriate time and people of this kind has to be manage with the some appropriate steps so that the individual that commit the crimes are warned of the consequences of committing crimes and it's results lead to dead and suffering physically and mentally as a punishment of crimes that one commits against other form of lives directed to the spirit or the physical part of the individual in this case we have to go ahead and take the necessary action to see why people will lose their life permanent; or temporary private form it senses and leading to pain and suffering, what we were about to find out about this cases, once it take action in some cases there will be no turn back until the process is over. One may say that god does not punish any one and that is truth because in life one has the understanding and the ability to see the good and the bad, and if you should commit the crime it has! To be conscience of the act against the other, and so everyone understand that when you commit a crime and it is deliver and know the punishment and consequences of the this crime and steel want to harmed anyone else sooner or later will pay for the act against anyone else or your own, So out of this we will agree that as human been that we are if you attend against the other you would not be welcome in his heart and will be spell from the home one then will be in out by himself until this man recognizes the fault and the gravity of the acts until learned and advised to do what; you would to do own you! Will do to others.

So that is the law! Because the law is the maximum authority and believes it not there are no mistakes in that part of the conscience in the man and the universe in full

25

Hi, HOPE THAT AT this time we all have thoughts of peace and happiness inside our most intimate part of our spirit and if we don't it's because of our direct and intentional behavior which is because the ignorance and careless attitude in our interest and irresponsibly taking more and more steps of danger in the life of others that could make the most beautiful use of what is the life in progress and the direction, some will take in the near future, it is very important to help and sacrifice for the ones in need and a potential positive attitude or one certain soul that may lose the precious gift of life and will be stolen by some other that could not act in the right of mind. In some cases the law will have to take control of the situation and justice will have to rule and make the corrections and act in behalf of those who will be at the right and have little hope for saving what it is left of a very long suffering and torture form of living life; in vane as we have witness that saw many crimes against innocent people victims of the careless attitude of the, ones should have taking actions toward the good and honest living that didn't take place while they were in power.

Now I want to call the real ones, those that suffer the consequences of the cold inhuman world of the most horrible and tragic real events of the life of mankind and the and the time very dangerous game played by some that will no longer care about the most precious and appreciated, the gift of life! For some been born is what makes a man a man and since this moment he will be called by his name and be recognize for his actions; and so living in the side of the law is, important because the act of losing his own life means not to fall in space en a deep sleep for the rest of his days in the darkness of hard to cope with, so please help us god not to fall in the ignorance of the monster that will steal our gift of life for no return will take place because the force of evil is strong and violent with no love to comfort our disappearing heart in darkness of our incontinence because no light will shine in the mind that doesn't produce thoughts and the images the gods gave us as the gift gave to us at the day we were born and could take us to heaven and earth and thru life as the torch that will lead us the way to eternity and will rein and shine In the highest of the mountain guiding the person thru the road of life...

26

Hi TODAY ONCE AGAIN: here reunited in and living the same issues morals and physical and spiritual, steel nervous and shake for the impact that mankind made when he was call to be man for God and the come down from heaven to disperse the seed of life in every place he has been called, and just because He was beautiful and powerful everyone at his steps honor him as he went by with gracious walk and his deep look point up front to the horizon where his site could' not see any further, and of course everyone in the forest that so laugh at him and his fine voices sound at a distance where they hiring, for some reason! And soon when he tried out from his journey and he could not see any more suddenly the big idea of a big fire light up in his mind and another challenge come to man's mind and soon he before get to dark rush to get the branches of an old tree and like magic after he has prepare got; the wood the miracle making them very surprise of the miracle of the light coming out of the fire and the surroundings were more or less visible! Every one say a laud prey and soon after that everyone saw the miracles of the mankind coming to put and to provoke the beauty of life in from of thee very eyes. That shines with this fire and when stray in to their souls in an effort to be grateful with this man, where ever he goes all the forest creatures bow in front of him because he cares for everyone in the forest and they would respect him, and from now on always was a fire every night to warm and to make it the power of world. Bringing beauty at every place he when. Very long ago god gave the world to mankind for the reason that man was kink and care about rest of the living been. All the creatures were friendly and loved him dearly, they when with Him down the natural fountain to refresh and to have fun during the hot days that's why He was never along at no time keeping company and having fun at all times. Soon after; the forest come more and more alive and the flowers gave Him a beautiful sense of smell and there color surprise His view at sunrise when steal dark and fresh since we come from the deepest of the forest we learned soon after end for ever to live with nature and we all come from nature born from the deepest and infinity space Man Kind always likes to look everywhere and at night He looks at the stars and dream about him and his sons that came later and we form the family and live for a long time quiet and humble in the town where we come from soon later our god has been directing us since we all left our town which we love very much since it was good and sweet to live in nature and the greater pleasure of going to where there were fruit and vegetables to bring hoe and with that the seeds where planted all over to enjoy for every one that come to town.

27

THE PICTURE OF TIME; comes and the number of hours mark 24; every morning at sunrise as a line pointing out from the center of the earth as there are mysteries to resolve but one thing is known that there are 4 main points as reference. In addition, when I get up and at night people, goes to bed there are changes in our life. The mind at work during the day is taking over; by something in the precious night, and there it comes in that stage the One! By him during this phenomenon call sleep and during it, the mind dreams like talking to him. On a stage of trance or time in which the privacy and the sincerity is all the way to top looking at everything happening in the internal been. In addition, the conscience and the balance and others take place to make an exam of conscience to see if we can find ourselves in order and happy. If there is something to correct is look over by the conscience in a complete overlook of our conscience where never can be forgiving and it has called the NIRVANA. Many of the prophets throughout the history of world, and so for when remember the name of god in His total harmony and peace everything comes to total calm and all knowledge. Peace and in silence of the universe that when accompany by the spirit and holy virgin in his memory tonight is a grateful night called holly night for everybody.

As we realize the importance keeping in contact with our creator and giving the law the respect and graces and the honor of master, the life for one is all that matters. When it comes to truth and knowledge inside of the night of dreams is the wonder of the obedience and rectitude; on the conduct of a human been having the relations with most high of all in the middle of it. The right things to do when it comes to the life we have inherit from our Gods in the name of truth and love. Honesty and justice for every one alive and! Hopefully nature will have life on earth as really the beautiful race that one's was prepare for everyone in our planet

28

TODAY ONE MORE TIME at lease think in the peace and joy of all; and since is the heart the center of joy and love, in our system; it feels like a sensation of intense and pure feeling and joy of yourself; of course is the wonder feeling and the realization of love personalize; in intimately love of the conscience product of rushing feelings to the heart; and giving space for more attributes to the personality making a stronger conscience necessary for the bean to battle the forces of opposite sides, in a been growing and getting stronger and to be the one and to gain the grades of education of our life in progress of; gaining the perfect life. Once this is accomplish we have the necessary values to keep his mind out of the danger of poor thinking and be able to overcome any of evil stages that take place in every one's life for the only reason, !of growing to perfection and to gain and gather the grades to become more conscience; and therefore to have the mental energy to make things become true, spiritually and physical capable of deal with many situations that may require power an strength to win the forces of the negative sides of a person, understanding that the evil won't tent the conscience that have overcome the obstacle already taking over, this is like a war that takes place in life to, understand and to become perfect, to be train for any situation taking place inside yourself, the example is clear in the figure of the life as a human that is born and has to grow and get strong in his first years to become; a young boy; training for a profession as something to make his life productive and to fulfill the purpose of his life, making it reach and a wonder !by itself and since then, life will smile every time you get up and confront every obstacle that he may encounter in life and this individual will take life ! so joyful and proud, because he has won inherited his own personality to live in the world with full honor and qualify to handle any task in society because he took the life serious and train to deal with the necessary projects, and the abilities of the individual to be self-sufficient when is called to his duties is what is called the level of education and the experience achieve during and thru the years. and so humans learn and gain conscience by practicing and learning from themselves; at all times depending on the will power of the individual in other words, a person is what they learn and what we want to be and do, all that we can do and since every one realize the meaning of the purpose of life we will do the best and no one would be left out, because the humans are like a supreme been capable of do what we want and be; but sometimes is difficult to achieve the desires of the mind and have to live for a while in suspense but not allowing the negative values to take completely control over the conscience of the individual. Making him captive and powerless to take care of him, and in immediate danger of success and progress...

29

THE SECRET POWERS OF nature, as we look in our surroundings there are many, many places to see and admire the way our mother figures out; in which manner? To handle life, in only one second. And thought the years are life for all, the coming and going of time, what and when to live The power of this is to keep renewing our life as one in a present time and for eternity, because we all were born in different times is unique; I think that the time are digits that we love and make us unique too; in the universe. In addition, with the number stamp in our spirit we can multiply and live happy because we love the time and ourselves now and forever go perfectly marching in harmony with the rest of nature's power. I think this phenomenon is like if the gods would had stop the time and then let it go to go alone with the rest of the powers and because this is part of our live have my especial time in my life is special; just the body we have too and all in one makes what we all are; and man and nature combine will live as one big family in our home make of the nature and had developed during all this time and the evolution that gave place to many wonderful material spiritual and physical to giving us all we need to form a home made from nature and for nature, sad that we know the powers of our nature and using them for developing of our home in which we will live as family and protect us from evil and keep love always lighted to be a man in power we must obey the laws in nature created for the order and protection of the one coming in to these world. Nature's power is for every one also a group of minds together working for our future and directing the destinies for a good time to come. Now where and what we are here is obviously there is only one way to go and it is forward to the future and the changes taken one can say has been good and every one learned from this era of transition from many times past and the hard it was to gather around the pieces there was to made a good home that be in according with nature development and the respect for the law establish in order to take effect and functions were establish to make the world as effective as it could were forever successful and working in order, since nature to need the laws to survive is ours to need of order in the system, and the assurance of life in the planet is more and more obvious in the modern time, also man had to fight for his life in a world of injustice actions coming from the no other then the evil and wrongly figure of the humans once forced to do what the wild law of most strong and most fortunate will do and in order to survive had to develop violent ways of living witch make him to violate the law and keep on fighting for his survival you know, and now never before most surely we see the effort going thru the mind, and with a sick body today struggling to survive hardly knows who we really are...

30

GOOD NIGHT TO ALL the participants In modern and changing of the present times, notice that there are many difficult times steel ahead in the constant random and perfect moving of the planets constellations galaxies on this most loving and beautiful place where we all eradicate from many years from now, and is so warm and fresh as the little stream that comes down the heist mountain always fresh and happy about himself because in its way it will find many fertile land to make grow and fertilize with its fresh water.

And now I say to all of you has been the most interesting tome in its own and perfect meaning of the no, one world along but many of them and so this life is real and clearly sensitive to everyone who is here to stay along the ones that really want to help and care for the others and himself because god's law it's the most heist and biggest of all in its own world which is law of the universe and for to glorify and adored and to serve at all of times in its own secret name for that is the world of the lord, and so today we believe in it and live for it because men has already decide what's the best way to wonder and the abundant and richness of the land of today, that why having faith in one and only one with the life inside ourselves which his name it's only known by the one, himself because it's the life from above and beyond having come down from the deep of the eternity to glorify god now and forever one with him and then for that is that men came from the deep sky where there were nothing but love and law and harmony of the celestial firmament that we look every night at bed time.

And so now we believe in the law and it's the life that reins in every particle of the universe itself because we come from life and live with it and god it's eternal life that comes out rock as it was water in the mountain perpetually running down the forest and constantly growing in its trajectory to encounter more and more life as it wishes and by looking around the flowers of the wild growing one and another time year after year like the river that is coming from the highest of the mountain.

And now that going in the deep of the spirit, we see life flowing from the been like light of the stars over the firmament constantly shining in the sky letting us know thru the eyes, the presence of life in everything we see because whatever we see is life and it is in front of us in front of our eyes, the miracle of living and the witness of the creation is those two windows like fire coming out from our eyes it is life in contact with the rest of the world what we see, by now it all converge in the origins of life and it in ourselves what we think and what we see everywhere you see there is life for the two witness have seen to and show us the wonder of life as it is.

31

TODAY IN AN EFFORT to take one more step in direction of end of the what can be the perfect future and even without knowing the exact conditions of the our living conditions of the future society, we want to give a surprised to everyone that went across on the road made by our leaders so that our sons have the same input to be brave and honor to be one more of the courageous to take life serious and as pleasant as it can be, and what everyone in our side wants is that! The same treatment and the chance to recognize to themselves and also bring out the best for his family and friends the history of his journey of the most important face of life on the start of our days once protected by their mothers and thought by nature in a way be productive and fine directed by all man who would be kind to teach and share with us the most honest and grateful thoughts in the way to Eternal life. The spiritual life, the world wants to be in this time of wonder and tenderness like is been directed by our leaders and real times in present dilemmas of the human been, today divided and at war with each other as the battle continues for the choice of many humanity ways of living. And now that the truth come on the earth to see the evil destroy themselves like an only natural way of living according to their beliefs and capacity of the mental system that is so important for the definition and classification of the social groups. At this point, we have the idea of Essence of life, which is to dedicate our time in things that interest the nature of the humans and the immediate relations with Mother Nature as our home sanctuary forever. And now the reason for a well-directed mental stage will be reward by the person individual who has conscience develop to help the recognition of his soul, this will be the defense, of any conflict internally develop, by those who has created identities that cause damage to the internal system making the person vulnerable to estrange mental activities putting in danger this individual health and making him a somebody that can be useless or even seek that may cause a threat to the future for eternal purposes and therefore leaving behind the Essences of life which are for dedicated to love and caring and tenderness of living.

32

GOOD AFTERNOON, TODAY I would like to learn and study about one or more of the nature's rare aspects of the creation and evolution of the world, and as proved in history nature; has been thru those systems during the time the universe started and began the process of progressive way into perfection, and for many of us the mystery of life is been one of the more complex teems on our minds, and so now for and here we think that one comes from a different backgrounds because some of people think different than others and in fact we act very different too, an example is the way some people think about god as a superior power capable of think, say and do good thinks while in life to the inherited world of happiness and wonders; as prophets of the past thought us in many way, for example living honest now will bring honor and; many think fortune too to their life, and in order of the years past the history has proven of the well been of certain individuals; has a very and plenty living in present, and of course the future time as we observe will bring them happiness and wellness thru life as it comes, and now the time is come for everyone to observe the behavior in the inner of the individual life and let us be invite to the goodness of the universal law and be protected by all of the group that make the constitution of our laws, and be part of the, that will bring us many of our sons to be the best in our own world that our ancestors with courage and a little patients they made for us, thinking in the years of life ahead of us.

Now and past! The world reunited in one perfect endless of time, the people who believe in what were the dreams of their ancestors is now a reality and come true, in every mind and body of every individual. some, that one day show respect and love for everyone in life and believe in the promise of the ones, that took care and thought in favor of the law and lived for one cause, of working for future as the teachings of prophets with so much work and effort thought us the teachings of their minds and the faith was big and their heart was pure as the a little run hurries to the ocean and then to the highness of heaven.

33

THIS POEM TO THE innocent and tender minds around the world and title it as cosmic sunrise, I have to tell how enthusiastic I feel now that the has been giving to the public and everyone has the opportunity of share his own opinion to the many points develop for the sincere and secret world of knowledge of the world, which most it is kept in the hidden places deep in nature" 'darkest places where hardly any minds can attend to reach and for that reason is that the knowledge is for those who are or has been through many tests for themselves and also based in his or her studies has accomplish superior grades and sincerely devoted to all protection and salvation and preserves life in every form for the world was created by and for every one alive and ready for work and to be ready for life ahead of us and for that the best of luck to this young people that are today in the audience of the world's today said in this lesson And may they be guide on the way that conduces to the superior and virgin dimensions naturally no one can reach without the previous preparation and training in young life as child that wants to be part of a grand and wonderful realizations of the minds in post to and to capture the knowledge but you will have to go in the very dork and returned with the treasure with you And so as we say the way to heaven is the realization and the capture of the mind ideas coming from our very private been and be capable of know the truth on every level and states of the mind as we think and realize the different sides and kinds of thoughts that come to the mind as this time for that is the mind the powerful and the sophisticated tool we can use to discover the secrets of nature but that's is not all one must pass the simple testes and an ability to decide any know the difference on the series of ideas and to differ from the right from many others hoping all time that this one the one we had preciously chose as the correct and most fitted of all and as man we have to be in the save side of your own private life in contact direct with the laws that govern the this world because in the begin of the day there was only one of them that was the number one because may be we were not only not born but there was no more than the universe alone and according to the evolution there was not the necessity of anymore because of the rise of the civilization in the pass on the present many others would fit in the complicated human structure of today When I talk about the civilization in modern times we have to put marks in the people that live now thinking that is hopeless and meaningless to live in a world full of surprises and for that is we never find any good reason to do good and to have respect for nature laws and we a lot of times take life as something vane like water in our hands vanishing in the nothing because who knows what to think of the facts that we live for and from nature which is the law and we must not forget that we do not live alone because of that we can love one another and to learn from our older brothers and our parents that we respect so much and will go to the places where there were no body but yourself and the law of god

34

THIS IS TO THE innocent and tender minds around the world and title it as cosmic sunrise, I have to tell how enthusiastic I feel now that the has been giving to the public and everyone has the opportunity of share his own opinion to the many points develop for the sincere and secret world of knowledge of the world, which most it is kept in the hidden places deep in nature" 'darkest places where hardly any minds can attend to reach and for that reason is that the knowledge is for those who are or has been through many tests for themselves and also based in his or her studies has accomplish superior grades and sincerely devoted to all protection and salvation and preserves life in every form for the world was created by and for every one alive and ready for work and to be ready for life ahead of us and for that the best of luck to this young people that are today in the audience of the world's today said in this lesson And may they be guide on the way that conduces to the superior and virgin dimensions naturally no one can reach without the previous preparation and training in young life as child that wants to be part of a grand and wonderful realizations of the minds in post to and to capture the knowledge but you will have to go in the very dork and returned with the treasure with you And so as we say the way to heaven is the realization and the capture of the mind ideas coming from our very private been and be capable of know the truth on every level and states of the mind as we think and realize the different sides and kinds of thoughts that come to the mind as this time for that is the mind the powerful and the sophisticated tool we can use to discover the secrets of nature but that's is not all one must pass the simple testes and an ability to decide any know the difference on the series of ideas and to differ from the right from many others hoping all time that this one the one we had preciously chose as the correct and most fitted of all and as man we have to be in the save side of your own private life in contact direct with the laws that govern the this world because in the begin of the day there was only one of them that was the number one because may be we were not only not born but there was no more than the universe alone and according to the evolution there was not the necessity of anymore because of the rise of the civilization in the pass on the present many others would fit in the complicated human structure of today When I talk about the civilization in modern times we have to put marks in the people that live now thinking that is hopeless and meaningless to live in a world full of surprises and for that is we never find any good reason to do good and to have respect for nature laws and we a lot of times take life as something vane like water in our hands vanishing in the nothing because who knows what to think of the facts that we live for and from nature which is the law and we must not forget that we do not live alone because of that we can love one another and to learn from our older brothers and our parents that we respect so much and will go to the places where there were no body but yourself and the law of god

35

AT THE ENTRANCE IS a mural of darkness made of black air it is there where the mysterious night begin and the wonder of these exceptional state of nature invite us to walk into it and go in the wonderful world of the known, the world of the night and mix with the night fog it feels like walking into to yourself inner side and guarded by the spirit Of darkness and by this been silence because no one speaks during this night so this is like been in zone of death and with it many mysteries of himself will raise up to the spirit of the air like the death itself but in love the man for its figure when he guards on the night and finds himself on the night in black but seemly the rein comes thru the nearest forest pouring water in all at its way and making even more saturated making it impossible to of keep on walking, there is rein and water all over the region and so the only solution to the it will be take cover on near tree with the biggest roots so that I can take guard on that tree that was by the road and heave rain make it even harder to take the nest step and the sleeper mad was also hard, and so as the time went by and no signs of residing storm and could only whisper to the brother in the about where comes to my mind but steel afraid in the middle of the night fearing for his life and trying to figure out what was going to happen to mom if I wouldn't come home soon but not enough

36

I HOPE THIS IS a good time to be next to each other and to stay in touch with the superior and divine world of the universal and side of law that we are trying to impose in the new and the almost encounter our evolution the, unknown universe in the process of the important and must be in the evolution; for the reason of our own well been as we encounter many situations of interest everywhere on this living mysteriously growing home. And it is true we are been placed in front of the law because is necessary to imposed some order in the human place of the creation and is been forced to assume the responsibility of some trouble passed, in the human history as we were in the state of evolution and also process of selecting of the same state that our ancestors when thru long time ago. And never understood for us the motive of the falling tragedy of all the civilizations and the reasons for it, but now more than ever we feel that today we are in front of law for some very important and obligation of the humans to report all our events of the past too and also bring the presence of the ones that represent the human race of today and be sure that no one will turn against the evolution and creating in these new world opposing the divine law and crating problems and impeding the evolution of nature and causing the falling civilization today; and so for all the race to become more vulnerable as we approach the line in our history that halt to confront the law and to revel the conscience and rectitude of actions in presence of the superior law, and so to be safe and to be part of the new world is the work we will be doing, to stop the suffering and pain and to put end of ignorance and sin cause of the falling of our civilization, just like the ones in history were completely destroyed for this monster that trap all the habitants in the big city once build for us from human work that took place during the evolution and rise of the modern civilization at the end of one thousand ninety and begin of two thousand years when the real confrontations of the evil was address for the divine law with the intentions of the salvation of the ones the new born and other victims of war in which they came to this trouble world, that is why god was once again thru the prophets send a message from heaven to the people and so he who believe in his word and follow his teachings would save by the grace and beauty of word that they spoke thru the them the ones choose to serve and obey of course the divine law and follow the star the direct them in the night of the modern civilization call to stay in the union and love of the lord

37

BEST WISHES TO EVERYONE in this beautiful planet for all dream and joyful to live on; because we have choose to come here and become man to form part in the evolution of our life and constantly changing and revolving world in which man and nature interacts every single day and during the time involve in the life of all creatures of the world and beyond the line of be or not to be, because is true that we all were aware of the different ways of living that involves the humans and the races of the world and indeed everyone thinks different form each other and for real and telling the true I would like to be my own self for the simple reason that genuine and perfect life for me, of course I want to be actively and directly involve in all activities surround me so I can be aware of what is working and not so for the good and the concern of and to be aware of the many choices to take ahead of life and of course it will be those; the choices of our own life and that is the life we will be living ahead of us and it will be known for the rest of the people surrounding and known to ourselves;

Once we came to the top of mountain and saw the valley I start to enjoy the fresh and pure air in the magic mountain and it was if I was the only one on this mountain; many thoughts came to y mind slow and profound in my spirit, the mountain was quiet and playful, and I notice a feeling of sadness because later I will have to return to city where I come from, but not with empty hands, and so came to my mind that I will study and learned as much as could about that magic mountain while I was in that state of mind and taking advantage of the opportunity at the time when everything was going and thinking well but I knew it was for a shore time because I will have to go back to where I came from, so I knew that time was running fast and the day I have to leave will sooner than I thought and so the right thing to do was to start observing my mind for any good changes to go ahead and do as much as possible while I was In the mountain, and the only way learned about the mountain was by looking around and admire the many wild life on it been the only company I had while I was there on the top of the mountain. Once I realize that all I had in my mind it was the beauty and the silence and colorful mountain all I have to do was to look and everything else I could realize about me and that mysterious mountain was peace and joy, and so the while I thought all that the mountain start to get colder and the air saturation was so dense, and the mountain became the color gray and white because of the saturation In the air but I did not want to see nothing else but this wonderful phenomenon cause by the water and the air in the mountain for this is what the mountain is made of a series of natural displays like pictures in front of us changing every time before my eyes and all I want to do feel the air and fog that is so good and refreshing to our system, and the could whether protecting us and bringing the spirit of sky to us.

38

TONIGHT IS ONE MORE night in this side and my mind remembers that one where any one that at the time was beautiful and unique because I only live for that wonderful night that came by surprise and with there was wonder and magic to, and that is not the only thing it brought, there was more than fog and darkness, there excitement, so that we could not help to feel love and faith inside, and soon ever thing turned black and white right in front ahead of us the wind was blowing peaceful and mother nature which is herself was saturated and happy for life was tender and beautiful over saturated with soft sense of the cold fog like the clouds made of the finest mother hair in the mountain where one day we left for long time. At this time I selfishly wish to myself that night never end, but about to get more and more saturated with mother's nature love and terribly sorry and repented for the actions we have commit during our state in this mountain and trying to look at the grate valley where I was supposed to get back sooner than I want to, so within my self I thought and which that wonderful night full of fog never end, but soon in the fog storm would reside and mother nature will come down from that state take a normal but not bad state and I have to go where the must call us and keep thinking on coming someday to the mountain where every day it's different and beautiful all of the time sometimes I dream to be in the top of it waiting for the love o my life to share a time with her and when I am in the mountain it makes me think in the pure soul that goes with me at all times because I believe that mountain was created for and from the god of the highest and finest state of minds thinking on only one purpose to keep and maintain the peace of the lonely riders that near the mountain visit it to get inspiration from the grate mountain that by night fall in love beautiful princess dear to go outside to take the fog bath and to be pure as the air they inhale at the nights in the mountain

Good evening, the reason of little comment is with a once again put effort in the recovery of the human progress and the help of the one other person that is willing to help others to recover and to amend themselves to the mission of his own salvation and the union with the one and beautiful spirit of world and to project himself to a more stable and secure future without having to be left along to the predators and to go ahead with the plans once made for everyone in the past not too far behind of us. For that, was the plan in the beginning of our ancestors and still is our most important issue of the present time as we go thru days one after the other and our minds still in danger of perishing in horizon of time so when somebody is to encounter danger on his trail of recovery and still close to fall in the dangerous and the terrible situation on the edge of perishing at the hands of big and absolute hardest

39

AND SO WHEN WORKING in and with the evolution laws one must take in consideration on a very strong and healthy mind to fight the forces of evil and overcome the most immediate and minimum require immediate attention so one more time is necessary to be strong at all times so no one can be victim of the falling starts and loose the bright and precious look of it fire seen for long distances, in the high of the sky for many people with having a moment of pleasure in the comfort of their homes, or children while playing on gardens where the plants and wild life are always working in their favorite tasks. And so like if our spirit stays alive and perfectly healthy will rein for thousands of the time that never seen to be old instead the spirit full of glory and honor wise and beautiful will go on and on thru the time one after the other like the rest of people that once obey the gods commands and went thru the road of recovery and all repent of actions of the ancient past once without direction and darken by the forces of evil that took over in the process of the painful recovery during the most difficult time ever experience by any man and his faith of seen the world changed for good so it was his inspiration, the gods wish to be save and to have reason on the minds of every one that was once very affected by the forces of evil strongly taking over the world and causing the pain and suffering of those that faith with the help of our lord and worked with the law to restore order on in a cruel world and bloody war on the planet already devastated by the forces of evil that seen to take longer than eternity.

On a world of dilutions is today the human state, and mentally disturbed we go every day seeking the truth about ourselves trying to encounter the real being in us because no one would be able to encounter someone else properties of the soul, and the others causalities of the person in us. And so man was call to this world to work with evolution and others laws of the Universe according to the process and progress of nature, in the past we only use very little of the mind especially the intelligence to work on the better himself and to collaborate with the plans of the global and original thought of nature begin with work over the recognition of the souls that were being borne without the powers to confront the world most notorious and primary issues for the proper surviving process and develop life style necessary to keep and preserve the human figure permanently and beyond as if he collaborates with evolution of the world in definite growing and developing with the most sophisticates and beautiful appearances of life of the earliest times of our life were life was about share with everyone else alive. As we prepared for the discovering and conquest of the entire world ahead of us, and since we share the same

40

BACKGROUNDS AND I HOPE the same destinies and fortune for all and the love of mother nature at it side we will be save from the difficult times that we may encounter in the future, not only to just live but to go inside of the deepest and darkest places of the occult knowledge of nature, been those the treasures of the grand challenge of our existence and as explorer and dedicated explorer and worker towards the secrets of nature wonders we were called to command over any other form of life provably ever been.

Now as today, we see everything more and clearer because of the emphasis of the man who put and dedicated their life to teach the laws of the constitution of nature as some pattern to follow for now and to make the world worked and to be with the grand and wonderful wild world of the miracle life. That started in the very begin of our life with a promise of going ahead with the rules and regulations that make everything happens and to protect and defend the little ones that just arriving from the genesis and the intimate side of the nature angelic places, and since the love is require to procreate and to grow we give thanks and praise to nature and one another the strength to go thru some difficult times in our life. So when to affront the present life we have a lot of issues to correct and develop the cures for it as we see the humans going in to the most secure loving and mentally developed capable of overcome the most difficult situations on road to perfect and mutual love, will be the guide of the children of the future and beyond. For that is the very promise of the lord and the prophets in action dedicated life to the teachings of the laws discovered from nature and put to work In the present and past of history and finally the approved and defined the applications to the dally life on today society for good and for the good of the son of man that is so blessing for the girls on the earth as this wonderful miracle occurs hoping for more wonder births.

41

ONE MORE TIME WE meet in the internal dimension of our mind and the conscience is present in inner part of our been, taking us to an extasis, totally in progress taking the mind to the action on the wonderful mental realization; in a state of perfect disposition for a moment of direct access to Nature secret dimension of the mind at the best of the point where one has the opportunity of investigate and get in direct contact with the knowledge of the divinity and occult states of Nature where we can have access to information of the secrets ad occult archives of the natural laws and its wonderful uses and dispositions of our world a world of mysteries occult to the plain and simple look of the eye for the reason of proper law applications in a world full wonders and the view is very much capture by the ones in a state of harmony and peaceful state of mind. Now we can try to find answers to issues present in the mind and of strongly planed, and so we start our studies of the mind with a pure thought the superior dimensions naturally grown in our soul and of the internal been, with a grade of conscience developed during our time in contact of the superior dimensions and mentally capable of reaching out for the knowledge after recognizing the truth and the positive feelings and internal dispositions of our minds reaching for the most wonderful and appreciated access to the secret archive of the universal knowledge where the information is keep and archive for our knowledge and spirit to keep to be the treasures of the mental dimension and perfect function of the universe and to have wellness in life and to make the most out of the life, been able of accomplish the tasks that required to go in the mental dimension of our been and have answers to the questions and investigate the motives of the actions in the time of life in the universe. And to have this information at the reach and access during life is what we try to make possible in putting the knowledge to work in the physical dimension, coming from our mind and then this is the things that qualify a man to be a wise and strong man and also we can say that the access is on the man himself the only one that can keep the secret knowledge In secret for him and others willing to go even further in our journey and into the divine and holly for the world is full of wonders and fruit to eat also we do want to go more and more into the deep secret of the mind.

42

SOME OF THE IMPORTANT points in the studies of occult knowledge are very interesting to review and this time I would like to mention some that has come to my mind and going in to the deep of conscience, using our mind to search in for more answers to the question in mind; like we want to know how does the conscience work and the constitution of our body were we are to live in; so now we want to try to investigate the problems if the mind is not working right or wrong, may be one has to develop the mind just like the physical grows in the Mother and finish his development all on his own then to be a man; and so we know now that one has to be educated and polite and useful at least at the point that he

produce all the necessary energy to be a man, a man of destiny and hopes for the live to be someone to everlasting and fluently life taking himself and family to the divinity and harmony every time you look up and see the sky, also known as may be the man one day took life seriously and conscience awareness enough to be recognize as figure of wellness a helpful and useful man as he was develop for the good and for the community an example of fairness and devotion for wellness of the spirit and his freedom to do as he like is more acceptable to the lord and he and the Holly spirit will rise with him to a life that will his family lead to everlasting and eternal happiness of the soul in one.

Conscience is developed in a manner of joyful and constant learning at his start. The mind lived to become stronger and spiritually, capable of doing things on an unusual manner. How to live, to live better, using the ability of the mind. Live better mentally and socially recognize for his acts and Social position acceptable and the ability to communicate with the rest which may be very valuable for others giving him the authority to act on his own. Planning your life for spiritually recognition to operate socially, privately, and public as well. Building conscience and spiritual strength to help others, improve living qualities. Approval of wealthy activities and practice of mind and body's youth.

43

PROGRESSIVE AND CONDITIONAL TECHNOLOGY developments to gain mental abilities and the practice of the Laws; applicable to man in evolution or involution Never before in the history of man; which is the one, that came up with the technology advances in the Modern time to be able to build the mechanism of the operation of machines, very useful and helpful on every project of the time either material, and building structures of the modern civilization, as we can see the on every day project man think first before start working on it. That is why we must develop our minds to be the spirit of the project and it will be a structure that will sustain the use for it. Now we the society to keep prosperity of the city? The truth is that our mind is in use and for purposes of advances either material or mentally and we can surely say that our mind is something precious for spiritual and the beginning out the new life, is the mental state that build the spirit and the body too. It is then life that we create on this world what our prosperity and our comfort in life what we make and the purpose of the intent to make everything appropriate to it use. It is then the human spirit the giver of life, practically speaking and now we have no errors, just like the spirit comes from above the dimension of the universe thoughts, what make the world, our world loving and caring every day?

So the wonder of Nature's spirit what made it possible to man; live in and surrounding the planet making possible the life on earth and heaven to be holy and beautiful for all Man Kind who believes on the higher power and to live for a very good purpose and dedicated to love peace and communal living for life is good and pleasant and our stay in this wonderful world and everlasting life coming from above the deepest places and occult thoughts of our minds of course we are what we think and feelings and mutual cooperation amount our people and ourselves been then what we are in the present and will be a future a figure most holly venerable of all creatures in the universe. Now that some good feelings comes from ourselves the mind is for us a wonderful part of a human been is then what we call our spirit the life we can't see and where the spirit meets in the holly temple to reside on us for everlasting life and will have the pleasure of feeding from our Mother Nature so we breathe to keep thinking and we eat to keep our bodies and to be able to move as the days comes and goes in the rapid of the modern society.

Once we come to the Earth sent to be a man to be in charge, to distribute the word of the lord and to bring good news to the people and to dedicate his time to live with the people making them strong and to gain the values amount the population restoring them to; original, and the most proper appearances and putting the knowledge at their reach with only purpose of getting out and reaching the heart of the population, so we become more aware of the situation and to be conscience of our own desperate situation in which we were under the influence of the forces of evil and control of the minds. This forces actuated against us putting in danger the security of all, for the same unfortunate past and the rebellion of the man one day powerful, but very inexperience individual, the negative forces were or had taken over the entire mind of all not leaving one, and so while this happen we become powerless and vulnerable and weak and at this point you can see that we needed the of god to be save and powerful again so, no one will have to go thru that devastating situation and with nothing to prevent the situation for the reason that man was one again powerless and weak, that is why God took part of it and especially gather the man to send it to Earth and go thru the same situation to see if they react and turn their life, for a reason that only they would know since danger was hiring and every corner of road ahead as we all must walk and since they were supposed to walk to learned to experiment with Mother Nature and feed from it man was in a state of involuntary and danger, because of course mistakes and later ignorance and chaos and dying and to vanish in a ball of fire and later really defenseless against the already developed forces of evil which by the way resemble, as to the very worst of luck and abandon because not body else could prevent the situation, since there was no other to assist them in the transition of an develop society and its only cause; it was to be defenses against the battle of the evil and to one day be in control of the society like powerful and honorable man, and now that we can realize the situation of powerless Man, and with no believes in God to protect and defend him from any attack of forces of evil, one day took over the day he would die, powerless and diseases and just like it became immobile and no strength perishing was even better so when we were able to go ahead with it plans and against the evil ! Dangerous and with or nothing could saving them with a very best law in every one.

44

AT THIS MOMENT WE are going to know some things about the human figure that appearance long ago -since then we had the opportunity of study ourselves deeply in our spirit and the origin of it, and everybody thought it was impossible to find then the true and the facts about the Origins of the human appearance in the material—physical form that came reality in the minds of mankind, the one that study this themes have come to the conclusion that it comes from the natural evolution of the world and this is possible but also comes as a creation of god, done by the powers of the mind or the spirit because the thoughts when are properly address become reality physically been able to move from the powers of the spirit, a wonderful function of it, and very much operating on the values of the spirit that are the like the desires of it becoming wonderful forms of life. And so that was the creation of our world a combination of sprit and material needed to use the power of Touch and the wonderful pleasure of the power of Seen amount the other powers. Now ten we known a lot of the spirit and where it comes from and the origins of the man as an important figure of the universe and beyond the frontiers of the unknown but now not a secret no longer about origins and destiny of this, the new man. For now we will proceed to the more occult places to find more of the answers to the questions on the way of a reach spirit and the beauty of man as a key to the future and wellness of our universe and relation of Nature Man working as one to make the world safe and more pleasant, because the figure of the human is now being watch closely as we witness the evolution of ourselves. There was one time in which every single person in the world thought it was no future for man meaning that the world was ending soon that is why they do not put a fight against evil just because it did not make any difference in this short and painful life with no one else to relay on of a ending life it was not possible for a man to go ahead and study the life ahead and so now on this moment the human been is coming to a more serious issues about and amount themselves for the reason that we will leave this world of ignorance and full heath for the reason and lock of love and justice, in a world of emptiness and so deteriorated to limit of not taking there only life more seriously at lease for himself. The minute we thought about the eternity and for the humans in the transition of the choice of live or die is now the time to decide about one or the other and the needed to time and to decide the consequences of a living with no laws and mind gold an aspirations to live ahead with the spirit of a good and hopes to become somebody in our journey thru life.

45

As I mention in the pages of this book life today has many points of view and many of us don't take right or the easiest to walk to road of life, and that doesn't mean this is way, in other words everyone has a unique way of life, always going where you which to go and doing what we like; that sounds right because we all have decide what you going to do after you develop and decide nest on your life ahead of you to keep being a man or to return to nature and live there or to become a more man than you are at this time on this state no one has the capacity of deciding of declare yourself as man for eternity. So now is the time to decide if keep working as a man or which means to keep the figure of a man or to lose the figure as and become spirit only to go in to heaven and where never nothing happens for the reason of having pleasure in this life or ignorance too or both because nothing else go or penetrates in a mind that is not capable of recognizing bad and evil from the just and fair and keep on getting and advancing in life because they use the mind to better themselves and to proceed to further places and to work for the constantly changing of the universe, as a director and in charge of his or her life of course, that is the desire of the individual in according to the population and authorities and rulers of the world. Even when Nature is could and silence this is a time for sit back and place the fire of the fireplace in good and example of the power that runs thru it and the warm of it feels comfort and joy of a new life a new day ahead and since the people like to keep a fire there will warm feelings during this time, and for hot season we slowly do the work required to keep food in the table and to gather the crops in the special place in our home close to us so no one will go hungry and weak and may expired in the time were there were no heat in the house and everything cold with nothing to do and instead be a season of joy and happiness for us. And as for the man who loves to see that prairie and the follower to grow in it is a time especial for them as well and when every season comes and everything has come back to the state of the flowering and work with this product is what I call a work of art and joy to those who really enjoy the prairie and it wonders of fruit and flowers in the planet were we all enjoy most our time and all the year will be pleasant and beautiful and hope to go into further places and more occult places of the nature in all us.

46

Now that time is reveled to us, the true developed to our eyes is for the people who must take the necessary solutions to our problems, go to top and from there, will see all the eyes can possibly see, and for the man is good and strong again the peace and the hearth will rise like the risen sun at the morning, and will keep the hope and the love will always be in the humble and quite of the hearth to, meaning that is those laws what will overcome and take over his soul with grate power on the love and ultimate the justice will show his fury of a lion deep in the jungle of fire. Willingly to power it and renew it to everlasting and as long for better and better, even if there will be trouble would not be harmed our soul and the light of the sun rise will always shine in the face of every humble and honest man that one day come in the name of the Christ and ever living god will guide us on the forces of evil rise and try to take over the conscience in us, and from now on when like watch man in the trouble and danger of the war will be alert so no more tears and cried and pain will fit in the temple of our god who lives and guards the people in need until the no more heath comes and steels our goods from us leaving the soul weak and vulnerable to poison and decomposition, seek of a jealous person trying be the brave; in his vane and insecure living because the fury of the lion will be upon this who tries to harm the delicate souls growing and growing to have a very bad wrong way of living, but instead the love will take over in the morning of the magnificent rise of life where no more living with heat and jealousy will rich out the one once; day were more vulnerable to the evil and the ignorance of the minds in a seek state that conduces to the destruction and provoke many disorders in the mind of our weaken society continuing with bad things happening in the mental human and Nature disasters that attracts the proximity of death of our city that smell like death which grew in the ancient societies too living nothing but the memory of the people who one day try to live with the sin and the violence, discrimination of the lower classes of the population humbling themselves to man and god to be one day hear and be the ones someday to work in the freedom of the world, of course this did not took place for a long time ever since the law was broken and the rights were violated and man's rebellion was first risen in the minds of the powerful and most notorious the one day long ago were the supreme and rulers of world and so after that there sere destruction and chaos all over the cities that were left behind since there were nowhere to hide and the fury again will destroy the city leaving devastation over territory were the population one day live and die to rise somewhere else and continuo the war of evil against god and the laws imposed for us which; we did not respect took, us down hard in the pain and suffering and death finally, and now we do understand the principals of a good living and to live off hope and faith overall to be with the spirit of lord and everlasting life thinking on the devotion and pleasant of life in the limits of love and wellness with no more pain and no more cried that harm our soul and our been in the temple of the living god, needed to battle the forces of evil in our temple; leaving us in a good position of the resurrection and to our spirit to heal to from our sins so we can accept the law of god and peace of heaven every day and every moment of our life and of course have the opportunity of renew our life one by one in love of the holy and grate spirit of our Mother Nature so we can one day come back to the garden of Eden where we all live and were born

47

Now AT THE PICK of life things must be going on the more concrete and identified bases for the future that is right here and now; and it is because life does not stop and the time which is the part of life in charge giving life to us every second and to extend and keep us alive thru the years; is possible to us thanks to the power of the spirit capable of constant and everlasting life and the mechanism of life in the spirit of a human is so exact that never missing in the way to eternity guide only for the faith and hope a man but in man ready to became more powerful and more conscience beyond the forces of evil that one day back in time was his trainer and his platform to the future life the tried to consciously aware of the challenge and willing to go make a little of an effort to gain the and possess his life and preserve it to his little desire so to help and be master in the human figure and Naturally knowledgeable of understanding the principles in Nature present; as laws of mutual coordination and cooperation mutual based In love and harmony essentially to keep the each other wealthy and comfort thru the years. That is how one does go thru the absolute synchronization of our constellation and groups of stars; living in a beautiful open space full love and full of peace in mutual and reciprocal accordance enough to let easily live with laws that are nothing but the product of our love trans mutated in higher energy and power to be the spirit that moves all of the universe, at once and hopefully forever. We are now starting to figure out the and understanding the principles of the birth of man and the appearance in the planet as very important and respected image of the most noble and more advance intelligent and capable to do most anything we wanted, there comes the issue that man felt to do what the he was sup post be doing in order to preserve his figure and the spirit of god which comes from the thoughts deep in the universe and the purest actions of the law concentrated Inside our own temple were every spirit live and shine I the name of the highest authority known in our universe we see every night when the stars shine give pleasure and which to live as time goes by and our fire will shine like candle light and it is what we know as the spirit and living human soul inside our body that at night he goes to bed dreaming of the new day where he will wake up to the new live day and to totally fulfill the most amazing things of our daily life. In the union of the our majestic place of birth we live with one purpose of whishing each other love and wealth and wisdom to use the power one day was provided by Mother Nature in the lord's name to governed and to go where no one has gone before with the purpose of realizing the principles of the marching and constant journal of our own life that fortunately was everlasting and ever loving home of warms and loving thoughts from our minded spirit living as man essentially to provoke an impact in the universe and home for the most powerful and wise man in and around the world.

48

I AM TODAY GOING to talk some about time. And the functions related, with memory, the realization and visualization they both combine and of course; is the knowledge the product of this functions. They all seen to have the common place of residence, in the perpetual rim of time in which are observe and place on to the spirit, to work with the been that lives, in the present; or he Is in the present, and from there; going back in time to remember what happened in the past and, is like if the mirror was the visualization of the images of the past. This all; takes place in the line of time and is the stages where the spirit lives and works; going back in to the past, present and into the future to reflect as a shadows of what he seen in the mirror of the mind somewhat like if read or seen and his images where brought to life once again in the present and return to night of to where they be stored in the shadow to be as our treasure of knowledge and conscience in the dark side until is time to wakes up as man of fire as the sun keeping from the dark he soon will start the day routings to keep active and tune for the day; now that wakes and the dark side is on a opposite of the fire and cover us now with the precious gold rain and the wonder of the activities is for us the sign of the wellness and colorful panorama we see every day in high of the sky like if likes the rain of fire in the highest. And so this basically our reason of the life is to be in activities like if we face the fire rain all day and ready for the night ; going to house the shadow would cover us with that wonderful dark and humid air in the system take over half of the day, that is how life in the universe restore from every day journeys going at night in a deep and pleasant sleep over night to see and takes the god vine during that spectacular of wonder night bringing us ever thing a man could possible want in life his home where he resides for the night and to meditate from the gods dreams coming toward his body and mind. So I think the night and the day is cycle of fire that shines perpetually in the sky giving us life for the good and giving us to the opportunity of conserving the our body at night for the nest journey of the day, to use it as we please and share all time with family and to go on and on to the end of time. Same whish for the winter days this is magnificent is like being in garden of Eden because the warm of the fire will keep us from many and hard days to come ahead of us is the house what like, home for the family and once in it be surrounded by this wonder of the winter because we love Nature and is exactly like we had to build at the very best a home for our bodies to be as comfortable and full of energy with that we breathe thru the window and our fire place be on a thru the night. And now we want to in order with the rest of our family and friends because this is where we live with Nature and the surroundings the roads to take us to where we want, this is what we are all thankful to the Lord God and beyond because where we live is the Nature as a big garden were born and develop to become a great figure in our times and everlasting life which is what we all want in life everlasting and prosper life to have fun with the family and friends living in one big and very interesting place

49

ALWAYS WHEN IT RAINED like to go where felt secure and as soon as the mind don't say nothing but joy and sadness and crying for the suffering on them, is when somebody feels like when justice is not done and the person that causing the pain in another been putting him thru severe and irreparable damage to him; one only wish that it never happened again, when somebody then put pain in the person who is already hurt is too hard to figure out why somebody would hurt another person like if it was the most lower and most degraded thing in the whole word that, means a lot to society and tell us, there is something very wrong in the minds of the population. Treating bad someone else is like if there were no law present in the human society system and already judge by the gods and the laws governing the planet it is absolutely wrong and vicious to even attempt to harm somebody it is not what the principles of human nature is about, so things happened at the early age when the mind is vulnerable to forces of evil at the opposite side of the good which always, is challenge by the people who practice and uses the mind to harm others; but as the Gods has promised to the good people the law will descend upon them because one day they gave up everything in their life to become the teachers of the new world a world with no crime and full of powers and love in a world where everything will be joy and happiness again. And again the promise of the lord is that the father who reins in heaven will governs all the races and all kind people around the planet in an effort to eradicate the evil and to do that it took a lot of hard work and because we gave up many rights so that some people may want to save and gain the gift of live in a permanent matter and be the opposite of the people who gave up the gift of life in order to have fun with themselves and enjoy the prohibit what is not food for the soul but is good for the body and having fun with somebody else suffering and misfortune and in order to maintain this state of vicious and illegal way of living without having have to be worried about where to find food for the weaken body, for they have gave up their life to have fun and to not see the big obstacle in front of this behavior that conduces to the destruction of the individual who has previously attempt against the life of another human been or the try to destroy the treasures of the power of nature itself for there won't be no clean water and no soil to plant food and or to have fruit to eat. And so right now there is conflict and punishment for what the evil is done against the good because the lord one day will eradicate the evil from the face of the Earth turning into a fertile and abundant towns thought out the world and to do so it was necessary to demonstrate these truth about the sore which turn against the evil who use it to harm and to commit crimes against others for they do not know the power of the lord and them it will reveled in front of them to see it with the necked eye and for some to late turn around and living their belongings and go with the chosen ones that will see and have seen in the past the future world.

50

AND SO, THE MOST happy and joy full in the year can be a day of this wonderful time; is any day of this sacred time; measurements guardians of our time. It is very well kwon as the living and companion of the soul and is call time our time so is for the mind a guide of our life, and without it; something will be missing lost in space with no point of reference and a friendly companion of our days also is like as I say, is a very important part of our life is like a component of the human system I think is measured in half of something, half of the year, the day something divided of itself that are connected and has to do with digital system, constantly processing digital data in the internal side, now there only one day but divided by itself it equals the same, and just like our sleep and awake in one day and one night which is only the same day; one dark and the lighted time which is the other half and together are what we call one day and one night speaking about this time I have to do keep me active and with something to do at all times so that we do not fall into the trap of the mental illness like disappoint or lack of something to do, falling into boring and monotony and possible mental disorders or mental incapacities as the illness progress with the time too. And so if one occupy the time in something good, the health of this one will be increasing ;in the contrary people who occupied their time with good activities will grow in knowledge and wisdom too, in any of this cases you have to understand that there is a third force and this one to be bad and all the activities will directed towards the bad and the individual will notice a lot of his passion in the crimes and in the all he occupies his mind for someday their life will be to affected to; but at the same time getting really bad is contagious to the extreme that everything he has done in life will soon come back to him, in the same way as the mind collapses into the inner side of his soul and possible very mentally disturbed and disable to point that death is the most possible choice in the future. His mind will suffer the consequences of the loneliness and will lose the capacity of interacting with others so that he will have no mental contact with others and will be enclosed in his own body. And so now the phycology has advanced a lot and since there will be cases in society that will make an impact in our minds but with the experience of the new era we will try to overcome the situation for good and a new and stronger civilization will rise from grown of the old civilization past. So now that the word of the lord has being hear everywhere and is in every mind of every soul in the world there is no more to do but to go ahead and wait for the ones capable of listening the world of the lord and surely change his past; point of view in which we were living like uncivilized creatures of the wild. And like never before we have to put ourselves in the position of the real and only one in charge of his life because there is no one that can save no body; the ones that fighting for his life have accepted the world and believe in the futures god promise us since the Christ came to Earth. Every one hear the worlds about the Christ promising wonders in the life and for every living being and in the most remote areas and a promised of reaching eternal and progressive life like if the men that come forward and take his life and directed towards, future in the name of love and justice will see the wonders of the word. The paradise fill with the essential fruit we all like and go to more occult places in this world and will be strong enough take his mind and body for the good and give it all to the lord. Or to the nature which is the same and to obey it laws and respect the others just someone loves the neighbor and to your wife he has to have some serious and well fundaments for; the law and our love for each other will see the eternal future.

51

I MAY LIKE TO talk about some themes which are very interesting for me and you. So when is the time and right place we can be sure that every day we must do everything we are supposed to do in the time we have lived in the Earth, and been longer time than others everyone is to do something against or towards the good of the planet and is pleasant and just to do what Nature would like us to do in favor of every body and for all that interest us and be good because if some wants to do bad this is being against the forces and the high power and will be more likely susceptible to live a very unfortunate life and also lose the powers and finally the will be disable and power less and more and more vulnerable to the forces of the darkness and the evil will take over his life but steel no one has any information about after death and the world of the involuntary punishment for the damage caused while been a man !and yes there are people how live in the world of crime and because the law give a chance to return to the a world of goodness and loving been in the planet to be chosen by god and live again, giving life to the death and to the ill healing the wounds in the body and mind, and yes the spirit; that- thinking must be corrected and restore to the way they come to this world, formally the law is actually a very sacrificing and loving people how only try to help the forces of the good and the power is just strong enough to keep fighting for what is just and to protect what is there as a father will defend his own son and fight for his life to, the truth is visible now is what the people what make the difference in the world and will be bless forever and that is exactly why forces of good today have won the battle against the evil and the bad spirits that come across every day in an attempt to make the trouble and the ones that will be in front of the law to explain his acts as the time is now and will be judge by his acts, and is not that the law will punish anybody however attempt against the family, is when they will defend themselves and the law in this case will have to act accord ally with authority and so no one else gets hurt no longer. It is so that we the people is can be bad, is the truth that once you get bad they will lose the natural powers and eventually will be a victim of the evil because there is not only one there are more there are numerous alive and the ones left in the world are in a fight against the each other for the reason is that we disagree is and the world full of ignorance and decadency caused by the forces negatively charge in a very dangerous situation that will! Take them to perishing and destruction of themselves this is what exactly is happening in the world at the present time better say a war. But a man that came from heaven long ago gave us the rules to live forever and gave the example to us and teach us the philosophy and the way to enter the kingdom of the lord and the to live peaceful with each other and is not impossible to become a good man in the name of the lord all we got to do is to be what we want to be and then the way will be open in front of us to head towards the high of the mountain and the heaven for all of us to enjoy the wonderful and delicious prairies of that planet without fighting and hating so much us sons and our ourselves fortunately with the new era coming and arriving with the presents of the gods from our celestial heaven.

52

SOMETIMES IT COMES TO my mind that things aren't going to well; for some reason do the best is all you can do, and concerned your own life it is the best at the time, when things don't go the best is time to talk to yourself and look at your been is the only thing we can actually do. Life can be the biggest mystery in our trouble mind because we do not understand and don't know what it is, well life is what we think what we do and what we all believe is our life, the things we think is coming from the spirit and we look like is ended the reflection of the spirit. Our mind is ended the father and the place he resides to be in contact with the universe and all people who believe in the pure and tender spirit will shine on for life is the most precious thing we ever poses thru the years and to the places we live in, is consider our homes and our most reach soil will come from it because we love nature as we do ourselves and that is the reason of love because we give birth with love and everything in nature grows because of love, and since babies and when one become a man is the most wonderful ever happened to us.

In nature and as man; to the process of germination is important to realize that the work with the elements water soil and fire and air to make the seeds germinate on the especial time during the germination time and so the rains come and with it comes the fruit especial the we feed and on time the plantation of the seed to make a baby tree so that never we run out of food to eat which is that especial fruit of the tree we are going to plant, now that we all know where the fruit comes from we must realize about the man who has babies and the miracle of life taking place in the our genital areas in which takes place the conception of a new life just as the soil helps the seed to germinate of a grate tree as a gift of nature for all to eat and enjoy the delicious of the gardens of Earth and so is the collaboration of one another what make us a family and all the love we share is the pleasure of feed our bodies with the fruit of the garden.

When the sunny season arrives at the middle of the year and prepares the holy land for the nest year and the light dries the grown and make it fine as powder then will come the rain and soon will make the seed germinates until this one becomes alive and in the way to be big tree, and now we must understand the importance of reproduction and the practice of the love rituals in the family and the love for your wife and sons for, is the foundations and constitution of our society. And to love each other as we love ourselves is what is in god mind when a great man is born from love. And so this wonderful world is made of love, understanding and beauty and justice for all.

53

AND NOW AS THE life of the ones in plenitude and the rise of their time bring all the components together in one so that the promise of lord and the gods to reveled everything before the light of their eyes and thru to the touch for the witness of gods has arrive in the promise land of the wonders for all to live, and to the enjoy and pleasure of the spirit that reins and lives in, as a witness of the thru statements made by the journalist of this magic and colorful universe that give us the pleasure to our eyes in silent and cool night they wish never ever end for a reason and unexplainable sensation that they experience from time to time deep in the heart and the soul of tender fillings bringing tears to our eyes and joy and satisfaction to our spirit in a body of wonders and gracious figure of the man. And so as night goes bye in deep trans we realize the importance of the behavior and rectitude of our actions and amendments and acts concerning the relations we may have to our families at any time we must cooperate with, and to make the others a peaceful and secure life so no one is left behind instead we bring the him home with care and love, so sometime their won't be the feelings of traders and to have instead a wonderful relation and interactions in family with the ties strong for the future and the hope of life to become one in our union and our progress for all since they all work on the developments and tasks to perform in our community, with the group organize and knowledgeable to realize the good and also the to know any counterforce that may have to be taking care of in the way to perfection and beyond, the forces that will oppose our destine will be only the solutions to any obstacle to our constant and the way of living in the universe and it's wonderful mechanical and voluntary actions to our activities, living for the reason and for the love, as a law that guide us to future without knowing and just believing in the power and the glory of the father our guide and our support of life. And it's possible to achieve the very and occult of the knowledge with the hope and the strength of the spirit, so great and so strong capable of accomplish and concord the greatest in life thru the lord and thru the love; making the people to go in the direction and guide to the future, with the only cause of and the reason of the sacrifice for our family and our brother, that became one of the most important issue in the past, because there was once a battle down in this same place and where we live in now, that's why Jesus came to us in the name of the father to bring us water to our thrust and bread to our hunger and to our hearts the comfort and the peace of and knowledge to our minds. So now we want what is ours and what got to offer to them is the simple and dedicated mind to put the wellness of our heart to them in and effort gain the step towards the future world and the hope for the fountain of youth and the blessings of our people to become aware of the facts that one can take care of needs and our most important things in life; so that we are the true and the real one that was advice to the hard work that we encountered in the past for the only reason and for the law to become real in this trouble world full of the danger of tentative of the forces of evil trying to bring the death and destruction to our life as we try to give the most accrued message to the world to make clear that life and death is only what we make of us and what we decide we want to be, in order to proclaim what you really are and where to live from now on to reach the sublime and interesting world of the realism and the truth for all; be clear and stray to our values of the spirit and the tender love of mankind once very propended to the diseased and weak.

54

MANY THINGS HAS CHANGE and progress during the time I have live after the time I was born, and now it comes to my mind that sometimes things aren't going the best but all I can think is that for some reason to do the best I can, is right thing; and the best thing concerning my life is life itself and it's also the biggest mystery in my mind and sometimes is ease to realize it, but is because everything in mother nature resides in the darkest places ever been and next time when, when the sun rays penetrates into this places finding the seed and making it grow from the grace of god and the divine laws of the universe putting one more time the glory and the grace of a new baby in this world to keep on to higher levels of life in both the physical and into the mind to be a great spirit on near future time. As for the humans when born and comes to our minds, the fire lights up making the wonder of the one of a kind with eternal purposes of our world make it' presence in spirit an corporal figure bringing glory to our family and happiness to town and giving the opportunity of eternal life to our spirit and be able to use the mind to realize and see the future In visions and images of the universe days ahead since we are call to be the ones once again to lead the way to divinity and power mentally giving to us gently to us. And follow the studies of our ancestors that saw and believe in the power of a great civilization where there were no more crying and no more pain instead of the of the hate and the flood shade we see on our world today. But now as we see around no one can be completely save because there is a long way to became a real human been with the powers of the giving and humble and justice for all, but the way will close ahead of whoever tries to enter into the garden and be impure because of the mark of beast that shows the reality of the spirit in the mind, from here on all we can do is respect each other and hope for the power of the forgiving and repented find it place in this world full crime and hate; making the place of birth pleasant and often frequent for our ancestors for beautiful flowers are grown in the darkest places of the mother nature when sudden there was light in it. Just thoughts in the air develop in the minds of the forges of the world and masters of the spirit at the time were where born combine making a man's life new and inexperience ready to learn from mother nature's secrets and abundances of the gardens, as the presents for all from nature and to enjoy the every time it comes around the every year, at this time when the new born are been brought to the world and every time there is a birthday to celebrate this anniversary one more time.

55

It been some time now and I steel feel like my life has not been change and fulfill because and for the reason that I do little, but when looking to what I remember what I was in the years past and even further it is not clear so I pretend to ignore the dark and cloudy in my past life, for one, because I don't seen to get anywhere when I try to remember the my own life as it should and I only assume that this happened and this did not happened all I can is try at this point think and guess about the what happened in past and I worry yes, but only me and myself can deal with my lonely life and I am working in my immediate need which is a task no one can do for me and as I think and something deep into the soul comes indicate me about that life is for the future at this time for the lord has said that one must trust and follow the star we always look in the zenith of our fully decorated sky with thousands of beautiful pendent making us going into deep love for Nature and the law of universal justice, and for now I will remand in this state trying to made everything as the has thought me since the begin of my life, and I do know for a fact that one's life depends on the faith and courage of our soul and wise spirit to thrust in case something goes wrong in my life is what I steel can try to work on it and try to fix the issue as I go alone with the stream of my life which is constant and always doing things to work on if I think it necessary and if I can correct my defects on time and to travel back and forth in my life time to keep alive and at least try to configure that can and do the right thing in the present and future because it believed to me that if doing good in the present in the future will be as it is now and this is a law, a universal law that believe it is just and fair for every one trying to go across the dark part of the his own life, which is not bad at all, instead is a training position of the person and a challenge for the spirit that growing in the time and space we all got to take care in life which comes to be in thru and in him that constitutes our life in total, and the minute one thinks in the power of the lord and the faith on holly spirit I believe I can make it to work on the rest of my life because I am a small pace of the universe having the same chances of everybody else and growing and developing the mind and body to become a real man with the chances of living with the spirit and enjoying the garden of Eden in many ways we can, especially when in afternoons we wonder on the roads in places that we like to be in every day bases and see that plants flower and the fruit of the trees aroma when in season of fruit make the area so frequent by the lovers and admirations of Nature's most beautiful wonders of the seasons of the fruit on Earth. And for our life I prefer to live in the future, working today to live tomorrow and leaving the trail of our life on the road of life, our trail that conduces to eternal life and beyond making everything for the hope and for the new life to come as we all grow in peace and for the good of our race that beautifully and wonderful approaches the limit of the divinity.

56

Now, CONTINUING WITH THE study lessons and studies of new era we will mention the theme of life in the state of virginity and the divine pureness of one of the three forces that runs the universe and the renovation of the spirit and preservation of the material as a element and movement vehicle and transportation of all bodies in our world connected to the spirit and the lord, keeping together all sources of life from interfering with each other and yet connected thru the sense of the touch in the dances of love and the rite of life as one. As I comment on the theme of this day I come to the conclusion that very important to dedicate a moment every day to exercise the acts of love In the comfort of your home just to keep the progress of our studies our bodies as the vehicle and media of transportation just like any other center in our system and natural habitat where we reside and every day of our life rushing towards the new world and a new life where there is plenitude and abundance and the knowledge collected during the past and projected to a very bright future and a life of wonders that never ends. And so as I think in our future and life after the death of our defects in us one comes to a conclusion that having faith and hope for higher and supreme divine laws of our universe is all worth to make a little impute in our individuals to be more and more efficient in the studies of any kind, since all we will have to worry about is to better yourself in honor of our lord and the masters and forgers of the universe in post of only a good life for all in the unity of our father the holy spirit and the son as one and the wonderful life of the future as a family and a good friend which in the friendship will keep us united for good and there will not be no more suffering and pain that we suffer in the years present and the immediate past, so dark and could as it would be if we did not take the road to educated and culture life in the present years and making that effort of voluntary and conscience awareness to take life very seriously and go for the most precious treasure of all the knowledge and life gift of life one day not too long ago were assign to us for the law and the most high that reins in every little body alive.

57

IN THIS MODERN TIMES the rapid flow of life is taking over the minds and all the thinking is directed towards the options of evolution laws, and the presence of man is a miracle from the higher natural dimensions and the balance of life is measure in it to evaluate the progress of the man activities and the way to follow in the near future, many has already taking the way the life after the revolution directed to infinite and secrete of our world in the direction towards divinity a s we plan it in the past were we live in constant work of creating the foundations of the new civilization and superior man hopes, and faiths to become a superman to control the new life after the final evaluation in present progress, to make a selection of values of the civilization that will take over In the future; and for now it is very important to work in our most immediate future, which is getting our conscience awareness and to be able to have the values to make the balance turn, and be strong to faith for your life in the future. Now that everyone knows about the nature plans for us, is big event and necessary to awake to the future life and become a man of divinity and powerful mind that may, and will be necessary to survive as a man this is needed and requirement to go on further In harmony with the natural life we all share universally keeping us alive and spiritually develop to know most nature's ways and laws to follow protecting and preserving wild life because as the population of the human race is now increasing the needs has already increased too. After the new era presently in activity we are fighting for survival and getting better too, so we can find space in the world for the modern man and the way to keep the humans strong to cope with the trains of labor and developing presently in progress needed to become the future man. From now on life will become ease and joyful with all minds directed to future and productive acts on the world of eternal living and the powers of the society in union with divinity and secret living as we all hope to have an eternity life in harmony with the laws of nature and so to become a figure of progress working to gain the position of a superior been and the effort to keep the promises of the very fine prophets in activity in the world.

APPROACHING DIVINITY

TAN PRONTO COMO AMANECIO el dia todo estaba aun mojado por el sereno de la noche y el frio hacia el cuerpo pesado y tieso que era duro de ponerse de pie, ya y para entonces la chimenea de las casas se notaban desde la distancia y el aroma de comida invitaba a uno a pasar adelante pues es de costumbre en esos lugares el invitar el caminante a un buen desayuno o al menos cafe para empezar el dia y seguir la caminata del dia. y asi fue como por encanto el aclarecio el dia en el valle al lado del rio que viaja al otro lado de la colina y asi fue que empezamos a caminar hacia el destino que tal vez nunca lo alcanzaria pues para el caminante no siempre hay fin en el camino de nuestro destino. Entonces es el sol el que va poniendo un calido sentimiento en el ambiente como el dulce de la miel, asi es uno no piensa en el destino el destino es infinto como la vida y es plasentero a la mente ya acostumbrada a viajar sin fin, y ademas nos enzeña a obedecer los comandos de la naturaleza que oportunamente nos enzeña el buen y el humor del caminante nos da a cada paso la valentia de seguir en el camino sin fin, por eso cuando uno ve un caminante al amanecer nos da una sensacion de obediecia al empezar la caminata del dia. Pero al pasar el dia y los pasos del caminante se hacen mas lentos pues se cansan las piernas al esfuerso del ejerciocio del arduo caminar y pues es asi como al pasar el dia y las horas se hacen cada vez mas largas el caminate tendra que otro vez buscar el lugar de pasar la noche una vez mas como si fuese un juego sin fin y es as que por ahi uno ve a la distancia la silueta de un a casa que no sabe si al fin sera su albergue y el tiempo de reposo para una vez mas el caminante hace un completo y un gran reto para el mismo, el de no dejar de caminar por los senderos de la vida.

En intento por ser parte de la familia de los escogidos por el Señor nos vemos una vez más en frente de los tribunales de justicia acusados por la corte de justicia y no sabiendo que el señor protege los que en realidad se han arrepentido de sus faltas psicológicas o físicas son un, impedimento para su sobrevivencia de los hoy y mañana un individuo sin aspiraciones es un hombre pobre de espíritu nada lo saca de su pobreza y no vive pues la vida; su vida se vuelve simple y no habrá más ni menos que los llantos y el olor a muerte y el dolor causado en el pasado como se oye de civilizaciones que desaparecían en el tiempo sin dejar rastro alguno de sus actividades ni sus costumbres y las tendencias espirituales que tanto necesitan los pueblos actuales y pasados creencias del origen y sus antepasados y así transformándose en una gran incógnita para los estudiosos del presente o cualquier tiempo dado; pero de cualquier manera hoy vamos avanzado poco a poco y con bases de mayor grado de seguridad y certeza más avanzada pues en realidad hoy hay más técnicas mucho más efectivas y con gran orgullo se puede decir que ahora se nos cumplen las profecías de los personajes mencionados en la literatura y estudiosos del pasado una vez rechazados por mismos hermanos y amigos de su tiempo que no pudieron realizar los mensajes de los profetas y adivinos del pasado, por eso yo no hay más dudas ni hay engaño alguno en nuestra mente por supuesto con las enseñanzas del tiempo. En realidad ya no hay más engaño y miseria en nuestras mentes por este caso y más claridad en la vista para ver los hechos reales de la vida.

Al día de hoy se notan las consecuencias de las acciones del ya cansado y más que nada la, contaminación del mundo atreves del acto humano; que día a día busca la manera de salir del lodo de sus creencias y creaciones pues El nunca antes se ha visto en tal estrecha situación y tan grande es la falta y la traición que un día llegara a ser preso de su propia voluntad y decisión en la que nosotros los hombres de la era tecnológica nos da un pase al más allá con las bases y con argumentos teóricos e ideales supremos que más adelante se le revelaran los resultados del trabajo en el pasado, ya sin vida, la muerte y la desolación en el mundo sumergido por la batalla del hombre ya revocado por el mundo de divinidades y la abundancia de los que en pos de la verdad y la divinidad fueron causados por los mundos del nirvana y el poder de los mundos superiores que cuando fuese ya la batalla vencida; no podrá ser engañado por los falsos testimonios del mundo inferior y las consecuencias de su pensar se verán el su frente como un símbolo de triunfante y ganador de los grandes obstáculos de nuestro gran viaje por el mundo de sumergido y doloroso tiempo; y más allá del sentimiento y la bondad de los que se atreven a arrancar los secretos y las leyes del universo que benignos nos dan paso a los mundos del superhombre y la humildad de los maestros de los sentidos que trabajan con la mente y el espíritu de las criaturas del nirvana donde se encuentran con el mundo del más allá fuera de lo común y el iniciado de los misterios mayores del mundo de los dotados por el espíritu de nuestro universo se nos da el bien y el don del saber y la satisfacción del entendimiento y la redención del mundo a su alrededor y más allá de toda falta y culpa se levantara la gran ciudad para que podamos ser salvos y la gran oportunidad de ser parte de la mundo de los grandes y maravillas universales en donde se encuentran con las bellas doncellas del paraíso en donde no hay más que amor belleza y vida por venir en el mundo de nuestros maestros que nos han de llevar al altar de la confesión y el perdón de los pecados y levantarse en el amanecer de la nueva era que nos ha de encontrar por sorpresa con los primeros rayos del nuevo sol también.

En todos los casos el más humilde y amoroso, se nos dio el premio del máximo, nuestra vida; ganada por sus muchas y duras penas que sin ningún interés personal se hizo al mundos del infierno y de vuelta a la superficie en donde se ven todas la mañanas el nacer del sol y la suave lluvia tocando con la magia de sus manos la fértil y cálida tierra en un gran y basto campo de siembra y la bella silueta en el bosque nos encanta con sus ternuras, y bien ya encontraran el secreto del amor en el huerto de los deliciosos frutos pues aquí nos da sustento para nuestra vida y la de toda justicia que nos da nuestros rangos y el don del perdón por los que un día caímos en el lodo y siendo así tan difícil de ponerse de pie desde ese lugar en donde fue el que nos dio la enseñanza y los dones de toda vida. Con ellos podrá el seguir el camino al más allá que pronto se convirtió en un interesante y fantástico mundo de amor, por allí también se oyeron los rumores de un tiempo de mucha prosperidad al través de la transcurrencia de la gran rueda del sansara que nos renueva la vida y renueva la tierra para tener nueva vida que es nada más que las bendiciones del espíritu en donde la vida mana como lo hace el naciente del rio en lo alto de las montañas, pues nunca cesara y de sus agua tomaran las más preciosas doncellas de la tierra y regando el campo rio abajo trajo mucho y encantado amor a todo, para así contar las historias a los pequeños que calladamente se agrupan alrededor del fuego para tomar una charla en la noche.

Y bien; para cuando el sol salía en lo alto y la fresca humedad de la noche que tanto bueno hace al rosal y en el centro de él, un niño durmió por la noche como de costumbre entre las sombras de los árboles se cansaron de jugar a los alrededores de la casa pues no podían ser vistos por nadie pues según sus creencias era prohibido dejarse ver por los humanos pues en esta leyenda ellos no son humanos, y en realidad eran medio espíritu ya que nadie había hablado de los pequeños con certeza, ya para cuando amanecía ellos desaparecían sin dejar rastro hasta la otra o sea la próxima al cual ellos con mucho anhelo; sabían ellos volverían en el camino oscuro y protegidos por sus sombras caminaban largas distancias solamente viajando durante las penumbras de la noche como protección de las malos influencias del hombre ya agobiado por el los años y el castigo de sus acciones ya no podía más y ni siquiera el reconocía su propia imagen y en el mundo sin escrúpulos sin perdón y sin piedad amanecía el hombre sin poder cerrar los ojos ya cansados y ciegos por los pecados del mismo y sin ver nada que su sombra él se va arrepentir en un momento dado pero nadie lo sabrá solo aquellos que tienen los poderes de las visión y el mundo de la oscuridad del espíritu del hombre, pues en si sus fuegos no ardían nada más el fuego del infierno se vía ni siguiera durante las noches el que no dejaba la sombra y no recodaba de sus acciones tan malvadas y sin fortuna servía ya en los peligraos de muerte con la carga de todo el peso de su propia desgracia y ni fortuna para disfrutar un día de buen tiempo. Así que cuando uno tiene en la vida el libre escoger y bien; uno como hombre tiene que decidir por sí mismo uno de los muchos que se nos presentan en nuestras vidas y como hombre debo tomar un camino al cual voy a recorrer por el que caminar y a seguir adelante con el futuro delante y la mente alerta pues hay obstáculos que sobrepasar en el destino hacia la vida futura y a esperar lo mejor de la suerte que nos prevenga de todo mal, pues es cierto que la vida ha de conducirse como un viajero que quiere llegar al punto de su destino y al paso deberá aprender sobre si en cuanto lo necesite y lo requiera su persona, y según sus escogencia en la vida después de su nacimiento y desarrollo se le presentara la vida como en la imagina y hará de Él lo que así El estipulara en su desarrollo y crecimiento del individuo, y desde que uno nace y crece no podrá dejar de ser algo en su vida una cosa que hacer y algo a que dedicar su tiempo en su existencia y permanencia en el mundo de los hombres al parecer más complicada y compleja de lo que imaginábamos en previos tiempos, pues para un hombre el caso es la evolución del mundo, el constante cambio de la naturaleza y la evolución del sí, entonces se cumplirá la ley de la naturaleza y el poder de Dios nos ha de acompañar durante la transición hacia el infinito y en pos de la verdad y el conocimiento para más decir que el hombre como una figura muy importante de la naturaleza y hacia el más Allá en donde se dice uno encontrara los poderes y la gloria del creador y la victoria del hombre sobre todo lo creado, será su fortuna y su dicha no tendrá límites ni obstáculos pues no más un deseo a cielo y lo que el necesitaría será un deseo de vivir como la ley y la buena fortuna. Y en sus manos la herramienta serán sus más preciosos tesoros pues para arar el suelo un hombre dedica su hermoso tiempo de trabajo, lo que más adora es el buen pensar y su buena conducta hacia el gran futuro pues es para nosotros el anhelo y los pensamientos de fe y prosperidad los más preciosos ideales que son la guía para su futuro y su destino será fuerte y como una fortaleza construida en el cenit de nuestra mente en donde uno piensa y planea el futuro que quiere vivir en un futuro inmediato y para así seguir el apreciase también ser ejemplo hacia el señor y su fortaleza vivara por siempre en un ir y venir del tiempo que ocupa para su bienestar y fortuna. Y al parecer la mentalidad crecería como un árbol fuerte y libre de otros que en tiempo liberarían la batalla por sobrevivencia y la evolución tomaría su natural curso en paz con todos los demás, así que cuando la madre natura llama a la sobrevivencia de acuerdo a su fuerza se cumplirá la ley pues ni más ni menos es para el allí a la sombra del más fuerte llama a la fiesta de la paz también en un mutuo y ordenado grado de evolución para bien de todos pues de los frutos del árbol de esto! Nos alimentaremos todos sin motivo de desconformidad y acuerdo para todos y por eso uno respeta el hermano del alma que lucha y trabaja en si con el deseo de superación y motivo de conciencia pura en nuestra mente y cuerpo, esto lo presenciamos uno y otro hasta que la belleza del gran paraíso se vuelva ley y amor para siempre juventud amor y paz y nuestro corazón del alma se convierte en un gran logo de amor y abundancia en donde ir cada noche antes de acostarse a dar gracias por el sustento y amor y ser parte de si en el trono de nuestra mente en donde se desarrollan las bases de la ley universal y futura fundación del todo lo creado y entonces ya fuera de su íntimo nosotros y todos nos damos las gracias por tu gran y preciosa existencia en lago de! y misterioso reino de las leyes universales, formando el sistema operativo del más simple y hermoso sistema de vida antes creado por ninguno y entonces se nos habrá de cumplir la ley en su orden y en fuerza; al ver un pequeño y hermoso árbol que crece con el sol de la mañana y por las noches estrelladas cubierto por las tinieblas se satura con el rocío sagrado de la oscuridad, en fin un gran y fuerte sistema crece cada día en nuestros corazones para que al nacer una nueva vida tenga su apoyo moral y espiritual y el amor de nuestra madre que está en secreto en lo profundo de nuestro mundo interno y la llevamos dentro a cada paso que en el camino hacia el infinito como hombre u otra clase de vida natural; así se encamina a la fortuna vida eterna sin el pecado ni la mancha de la sangre que no nos deja en paz día y noche con la espada apuntada hacia el corazón de nuestra madre donde reside y reina pues el que atentase contra esta se llenara de odio y lujurias que más en el camino del rio que viaja hacia el gran océano se secara antes de conseguir el destino y el fuego del astro solar lo secara y para entonces su cauce, en el camino al amor y la sobre vivencia se presentaría y cumpliría la ley, la más grande de todos los tesoros del alma se desvanecerán sus dejar rastro de ninguna clase ni sospechas de que allí un día vivieran por allí. Para entonces y con la nuestro anhelo de la partida hacia el mundo de amor y la justicia ya se hará su presencia en lo alto de la montaña que un día nos vio nacer en el cómo escondiéndose de las fieras del bosque, cuando nadie lo esperaba; con el cielo estrellado nuestra madre e hijo vino al mundo. Y dentro de poco su presencia se notó, En pueblo abajo al pie de la montaña que dio a luz el día de la creación del hombre y entonces uno puede seguir el camino de Dios o puede seguir el camino del que no fue, el que por una u otra causa se revelo contra la ley y la vida a sus alrededores fueron los deseos los que lo llevaron a su revolución contra el sistema de orden y control de vida lo que no pudo con su mentalidad ya manchada por el pecado y la sangre del hermano cuando uno fue caído por el rayo desde lo alto que a veces parecía venir de la montaña y por allí se oyen los rumores de muchos que no tuvieron la capacidad de seguir el camino del sagrado corazón de Jesús con que el dio al mundo la luz de amor y paz para así enseñar al mundo la verdad y el poder de Dios, nuestra mente que ilumina el sendero de la vida hacia el infinito donde encontrara el tesoro del viajero que no se cansó de la búsqueda del gran y afortunada vida eterna. Ahora para cuando la luz del día nos despertase en lo alto de la montaña nuestro y el deseo de ver un día nuevo al instante de que uno abra los ojos se nos concede la gracia de verlo y sentir su calor también y uno piensa de que pasaría si uno no abriera los ojos! No vería la luz del sol, Lo más precioso del día que uno como niño se le alegra tanto en el amanecer del día pues necesario para la subsistencia y el alimento espiritual de todos y cada uno de nosotros los que vivimos aquí y por allá pues sería la maldición más grande y penosa para nosotros no ver el arroyo que corre y también nos sería imposible seguir el gran transcurso del día donde la luz es la Ley y en la noche la oscura penumbra es el amor materno como jugando con su hijo en la cama, lecho de amor que tanto bien nos hace para seguir el camino del Dios del supremo y Ley del universo con las manos arando el terreno donde se procesan la nueva vida y el producto del amor se nos presenta como las manos fuertes del labrador de la tierra que siembra para su sobrevivencia y subsistencia de su familia y por amor a sus hijos y esposa toma su herramienta y cada mañana al salir el sol se le ve como una silueta de humildad en el camino al campo en donde se producen las frutas que antes fueron ideas en su poderosa mente y queriendo hacerlo realidad se llenó de amor por su esposa e hijos los cuales aprenderán del padre sus oficios del día y por la noches frescas como incitando al amor y bien protegidos por los enemigos del amor se esconden en la oscuridad asechando los demás para así tratar de matar los que al bosque del lago encantado se refieren al amor y la paz sean destruidos, pero no aun y sabiendo el hombre de bien el explorador del íntimo y amo de si con el estudio y el trabajo se abre paso hasta los lugares de oficio sagrado en donde se ven con la justicia interna y nos cuentan que sus aspiraciones de ser hombre, un tras endentado de los misterios mayores y sus deseos y sus poderes del natural, hombre de bien y por todo los que en el confían los lleva y los guía al arroyo donde encontraran aguas; frescas para saciar su sed y tus cuerpos limpiar! Al mismo tiempo tener un bonito y agradable tiempo consigo mismo y su mente con sello de hierro mantenía su persona con rectitud in autoridad de león y su mirada profunda revelaba su gran conocimiento se hombre que construye sobre la simiente solida donde no cabe la menor duda de traición y es siempre fiel a su esposa que profundamente se ve haciendo sus quehaceres del hogar. Y como un jardín en flora las aromas que salen invitan a permanecer cerca en ella y por supuesto el color de la piel era como la miel creyendo ser la más amada del mundo, durante el tiempo invierno la flora se mantenía verde como la esperanza del floral que pronto llegara y en su presencia ella se satura del hermoso aroma de su jardín, y es así que uno por las noches descansa de las faenas del día para que el cuerpo reposar y renovar la salud del físico y la mente se sumirá en un sueño profundo del alma y disfrutando de si hay actividad íntima y nadie más es el uno con quien uno con el que habla con el disfruta también de las actividades del propio y se humedece el mundo interno del hombre, entonces es como un sueño de muchas horas de duración y uno no quiere que pasara la noche en cuanto dormimos. en instantes de mucha placer en corazón y la mente fuese un como poderoso instrumento de comunicación que nos invita a la charla de los enamorados y el amor por su esposa se hizo inmensamente grande y tierno al momento de la llegada de la noche y los misterios del amor también!. Entre tanto el clima cambiaria y pronto las hojas de los empezaban a secar por color de la entrada al próximo verano muy seco y cálido por eso los niños van en esos días a jugar con las pelotas en la plaza del pueblo y con toda y todo los juegos de nuestra cultura son algo muy y grande para nosotros pues con ellos la mente puso aprender de los negocios de la comunicación con todos y cuando un niño se nos presenta y nos invita a jugar a la pelota muy contento Él se hace al campo en donde se juega a la pelota, pues es importante seguir los amigos del pueblo y la socialización nos ha de invitar a la fiesta del amor, a la cooperación de hombres y damas del pueblo que con alegría se hacían al centro del pueblo para participar en la fiesta. Pronto se vieron las señales d nuestro amor por las cosas de la convivencia de la familia sin él; sin motivo de ser el uno para el otro pues es también necesario y justamente de acuerdo los amantes se ven envueltos en un gran y admirable respeto por uno al otro. Pero entre tanto miremos ciertos fundamentos de ser hombre; uno tiene el deber de superarse, ser luchar por ser feliz pues cuando uno vive en el bien será feliz y caminara hacia donde su conciencia ve; en tanto que tiene experiencia, el camino del destino le dirá en el oído los secretos del viajero que se deja llevar por su guía y sus tantas experiencias y casos reales le harán su sabiduría y amor y entendimiento para los llevarlos sin problema alguno a sus destinos, para que un día los que saben el camino a lo alto de la montaña de ida, de regreso también solamente así un hombre podrá ser y obtener el conocimiento y el verdadero milagro de la realización y la perfección en donde uno se guarda de muchas batallas que liberara en cuanto uno viva y exista en este mundo sin fronteras ni límites para la mente humana, pues eh!ahi que la enseñanza nos protege y defiende como un león en la selva, es la espada de los jueces y los hombres de bien. Por ahí se oyeron los rumores de que ellos nunca hirieron los sentimientos ni el amor de su esposa ni otro hombre ellos insultaron en su presencia tampoco se aprovecharon de sus hermanos cuando estaban en necesidad, en cambio ayudaron a todos ellos y fueron testigos fieles del bien cuando por una u otra razón se vieron envueltos en apuros y ya cuando alguien enfermo así se dieron la mano para su auxilio y sus heridas fueran sanas, así que para ellos son muchos los casos del injusticia y de ninguna manera fuese herido de muerte y por los falsos testimonios, en cambio la belleza fue su enamorada y su poder se dobló ante la presencia de las doncellas que por ahí frecuentaban las riveras del rio para ducharse en las orillas del rio siendo el testigo de un amor que vive en el hasta el final tiempo sin desvanecerse por su edad ni sus actividad de trabajo más bien se ha de rejuvenecer con El. Así que nosotros hoy fuimos de paseo al huerto donde abundaban las nueces y frutas para que la fiesta del trabajador le diera la satisfacción del hombre de bien. Entonces para nosotros los que aun dudamos del poder del hombre y la belleza de su persona al mirar sus ojos uno puede decir que ha visto la esperanza de ser como él y poder servir con honor su persona que se fue a un lugar lejos de aquí con la esperanza de hallar el tesoro de vida, Sin ningún problema en el camino que se le fue hecho a su paso y vio que su gran promesa de ir a esparcir la semilla del Cristo cuando aun siendo joven sus enseñanzas se hizo al campo donde encontró muchas incógnitas de serios problemas que tenían las razas humanas en pueblo de la fiestas y la alegría se apoderó de El cuándo se le fueron las puertas abiertas por los que le esperaban a la fiesta y a su paso las doncellas del pueblo le adornaron con flores y perfumen e incienso para su gloria. Así entonces diremos a estos que el tiempo y la vida nos dará la gran bienvenida al pueblo que siempre fue muy querido por ellos y en secreto sus manos se hicieron al trabajo del campo y la más querida ambición se le concedió como el milagro de la vida misma. En tanto esto pasa en este mundo de fenomenales y grandiosos ya demás hay muchas cosas que debemos tomarle importancia y trabajo directo en momentos como estos, son muchos aspectos de que nosotros debemos tratar y cuando sea posible vivir con la mente alerta y un cuerpo entrenado para librar cualquier tasca que se le presentase en un momento dado, así pues se puede decir que estamos propensos a caer en asunto que fuese dominante y ante este asunto uno podría cometer errores también y entonces usaríamos procedimientos a seguir por el comino que nos conduce a la salvación de nuestra persona, tan importante es que uno se recupere de los ataques del ego, el sí mismo que latente permanece en nosotros para que el hombre siga la lucha contra el mal, contra los obstáculos del camino que nos ha de a conducir al triunfo de la vida eterna y la sabiduría del individuo más uno siempre alerta debe tomar las precauciones del caso a seguir y seguir tratando de llegar a la perfección del mental como el mediador entre espíritu y físico entre lo divino y el material de que somos y que tanto nos ha costado conseguir en la lucha por ser parte de la raza humana como nuestra familia y amistades del globo. Para este momento se debe uno hacer al campo y ver desde allí los procedimientos a seguir en pos de la lucha por permanecer en el físico y continuar hacia el infinito lo cual uno como hombre debe analizar debe comprender y una vez realizado en la mente como un poder de gloria para nosotros nos ayuda a distinguir y reconocer nuestros errores y nuestra batalla contra nosotros mismos como un gran entrenador para la supervivencia en el mundo físico y espiritual entre el nacer y evolucionar en pos de la meta que es el mantener el cuerpo y espíritu juntos en un armonioso ir y venir del tiempo que es tan pacido como el aire fresco que respiramos y manteniendo el equilibrio nos da el conocimiento para poder ser un hombre superdotado e inmortal pues es el espíritu de nosotros vivirá entre nosotros por largos tiempos además, con la mente como medidor se nos da la gran oportunidad de pasar al mundo sin fronteras en donde encontrara la grandeza y la bella natura que dulcemente nos acoge en su manos y nos dio el sustento cada instante que respiramos el aire de las montañas y los frutos del jardín, así que cuando bebemos el agua del rio y para saciar la sed damos las gracias por tal acto y entonces recibiremos las bendiciones del señor y en tanto nosotros proseguimos por el camino que conduce al luz de la mente el inteligente que a tomo el tiempo para así estudiar y analizar los chances de poder y tener la gracia de pertenecer a la familia del hombre y el amor de sus hijos lo llevo hasta su hogar en donde todo sería humildad y amor conocimiento y gloria etc. Y así que cuando la tarde llega y sol se oculta la noche se aproxima para restablecer el cuerpo y dejar la luz del día nosotros pasamos por el fenómeno de la restablecido corporal y pues también el proceso del pensamiento al dormir y para luego cuando por noche el individuo sueña, se imagina en el mundo de los sueños dentro de sí mismo hablando y haciendo cosas de la imaginación en el tiempo, en la mitad de la unidad que al unirse será el uno, que es la imaginación y el pensamiento uno actúa durante la noche y el día trabajando juntas una tras la otra se formara el cuatro estados de la vida inicial en un y constante ir y venir del tiempo, así es que tenemos el tiempo el espacio donde la materia se encuentra y con el espíritu para juntos vivir y pensar y con la imaginación hará sus sueños realidades del que más adelante ira a beneficiarse y ser el que en una u otra forma consiga la eternidad del espíritu ilimitado y lo que hubo imaginado se convirtió en realidad gracias a nuestro espíritu en el cuerpo donde de ahí ira a despertar a un nuevo día ;no será el mismo porque el ayer el paso al más allá y vivirá en nosotros por largos tiempos por venir hasta el fin del tiempo y los elementos naturales formaran su hogar donde va empezar la exploración, la realización del vivir en el hogar y nuestro lecho de amor junto a todos los demás para que un día de tantos se nos haga un milagro el de ver todo las maravillas del cielo de donde vienen todos los seres de las tinieblas y de la luz de donde viene todo lo creado para nacer una vez en las penumbras de la noche y para ver el día al abrir los ojos por primera vez. Y entonces como las imágenes se transforman en el centro psíquico y deben tener un significado especifico en la mente donde son procesados y analizados en el mundo espiritual que vive en el todo ser y nos da el poder de hacer lo que en la mente se procesaría y se ejecuta y personaliza también en lo íntimo del ser el cual es que da poder al físico y nos da vida y ve que al pensar al transformarse en moción nos movemos por camino al hacia el destino que ha sido procesado en nuestra mente pues con este poder nos ha beneficiado el cielo del nuestro señor que son leyes del universales y el amor de espíritu nos mantiene en el cauce para no ser perdidos en el tiempo pues nuestros ojos no verán la luz y el amanecer ni tampoco se ve el cielo con infinitas estrellas y profunda admiración por la belleza del firmamento, así pues tenemos que nuestro origen de las profundas intimidades del universo y siempre puras provienen de la energía psíquica universal para nuestra sorpresa el espíritu del hambre es si este mismo; al igual que todo tiene su propio sistema de pensar o su especifico línea, o de pensamiento que lo caracteriza de los demás y le da la independencia y la pureza de su alma que mora y reina en todo lo creado y entonces es cuando el que tiene la conciencia despierta y los sentidos en operación podemos decir que es o ha llegado a ser un hombre el que más tarde se verá envuelto en muchas situaciones que son la escuela del individuo en donde el aprenderá y se lanzaría hacia la perfección pues como todo ser al nacer; crece se desarrolla y aprende de si cada paso que él toma como un bebe aprende a caminar y más adelante tendrá que decidir entre muchas y e intrigantes situaciones que nos evaluarían día tras día en un incesante cambiar del tiempo y nos ha de dar la salvación y vida eterna ;tan codiciada por especialmente los hombres que vivimos en las penumbras del amanecer de la vida que hace unos siglos hubo empezado y creado por los elementos de la naturaleza madre de todos y hogar en donde será nuestro sustento en todos los tiempos y porvenir futuro; el futuro que todos esperamos con tanta ansiedad lo esperamos tratando de ver las señales que en tiempos pasados nos dieron los profetas y los guías del mundo. En todo caso el hambre apareció en la penumbra de la noche y en tanto continuemos con la lucha de los temas que se procesan en la mente y uno no los ha de hacerlos reconocidos como lo que en realidad y de verdad el significado de estos no avanzaríamos en el transcurso de los días delante y cuando sucede uno no evoluciona en la vida como hombre y entonces viene a nosotros tiempo girando sin cesar y las leyes naturales no las reconocerá tampoco lo que viene a ser el mayor obstáculo para la transición de los que hoy han caído en la duda y el error y en profundo sueño del que nunca más despertara pues será inútil ya que sin reconocer el bien del mal nadie puede ayudar al que nunca se preocupó por estudiar o dedicar su tiempo al trabajar sobre si sin tomarle la atención requerida al error y la caída del hombre, por su propio e ingenuo pensar que nunca se reconoció ni pudo en el mundo la vida sagrada pues sus quehaceres dedicados a los errores cometidos por las mentes que no reconocían el bien del mal ni tampoco dieron la esperanza de esfuerzo y superación para ser parte del futuro que se mira tan agradable desde la penumbra de la noche pues al despertar en la mañana habrá felicidad y sabiduría del hombre no pasara sin notarse pues para el que trabaja y vive con las leyes de Dios será protegido por leyes que son los pasos a seguir hacia el futuro cercano. No tan lejos estará la meta propuesta por los hombres de buena fe con la verdadera sabiduría; la de sacar la humanidad de las penas del crimen y el sufrimiento que no es otra que la pena de los pecados en pleno día, al seguir por el camino de los placeres del pecado; y por lo tanto su más ignorante practica de los infra-sentimientos en donde el hombre solo piensa sin tener la menor idea de los significados del acto cometidos durante el proceso del pensamiento y acciones cometidas durante el proceso; pues eh! Allí que el hombre es exacto y preciso lo que piensa pensando y actuando erróneamente de por vida causando su propio destino en pleno día y por la noche vera el despertar del nuevo día sin arrepentirse de los crímenes que cometiese durante el ya ido día sin provecho alguno pues el, ya poseído por las entidades de su propia persona se caería en el inmenso mundo de los sueños despiertos que cometiendo actualmente se ira alejando hacia lado opuesto y lejos ya del nuevo día. Y entonces el tiempo no quedara marcado ya que no vera el nuevo día por nacer y sus hermosos rayos de amanecer en un eterno florecer de todos y cada uno de los amaneceres a la vida tal como la viéramos en el cenit del firmamento. Dónde las estrellas de nuestro profundo sueño vieron los profetas de todos los tiempos y hasta ahora no hemos visto ninguno salir avante con sus extremadas equipaje para el viaje hacia lo más profundo de nuestro ser. En donde uno no puede ver sino con la luz del nuevo y por eso y más la fe y la esperanza de ver sus sueños hechos realidad saliendo a la luz del nuevo día saliendo de la oscura noche para darnos un día más de nuestra vida y la existencia del alma sin temer a los rayos del sol cálidos y amigables podríamos del nuevo y seguro amanecer. Donde la luz revelaría los secretos del presente y los testigos que fueron leales al deber de hacer la verdad resalir al día nos han de llenar de compasión de felicidad hasta el final del tiempo, y para que la creación fuese el gran éxito de la nueva era del conocimiento objetivo y leal a los hambres del pasado también es nuestro el camino hacia los lugares secretos en un momento dado los nos habrán revelar los más incognitos e indecibles de las conocimientos a ser descubiertos, en el trayecto a los más y más desconocidos lugares del universo, pero antes nos darán las claves de la prosperidad y el buen vivir aquí en nuestro planeta en donde la batalla de ser; para los humanos sigue tomando lugar en estos días de tanta confusión y desorden sociales pues son sus indecibles los estados de la moral en que todos nos impide la transición hacia los lugares de más y más abundancia y conocimiento que nos hablan los que realizaron quienes un día vieron el futuro del mundo en el cenit del día y por las noches su mente se llenaría de gloria y jubilo cuando vieron los secretos más complicados del universo trasformado en muchos lugares que en sus horas de placer nos dio medios de poder conocer la verdad y la justicia para sus usos en el futuro, pues es sabido que cuando no hay más pecado en la mente no cabra error alguno en el futuro, es por eso que la mente acostumbrada a estudio y el buen uso no abra más sufrimiento tampoco lo que en el pasado fue muy doloroso la transición a las dimensiones superiores tomadas por sorpresa cuando aún el día no daba las señales de un gran y nuevo amanecer al futuro sin necesidad de el error y las leyes del mundo se nos han de mostrar con suprema claridad para felicidad de todos los que en ellas creyeron y sus vidas dedicaron a cumplir el mandamiento y su respeto por las leyes universales les protegieron desde ahora y por siempre el hombre se vio envuelto en las más interesantes y gloriosos estudios sobre todo el no tendrá miedo ni dolor que lo rechazará en momentos de necesidad y ayuda para qué es más, sea protegido y glorificado desde el cielo cuando El miro todo el firmamento y más. Y así el agua que mano del cielo en ese momento al acostarse el sol y las tinieblas invadieron la atmosfera, los vientos nos querían decir que venía un tiempo de lluvia severo; pero no sabíamos que tal grado de fuerza traía la tormenta ; y la caída del agua empezó pronto; sin esperar mucho la lluvia empezó pronto, sin esperar mucho como perlas cayeron del cielo pues son preciosas; como si Dios derramara un cántaro sobre la tierra, pensando en todos los que de la lluvia se beneficiarían y cuando cae las madres se alegran y también los niños a jugar salen de sus casas celebrando el día en que la lluvia venía con un mágico canto de amor y paz; una vez que llego la lluvia a ese lugar trae consigo la bendición como regalos a los que con ella se identificaran y hasta Él se alegró de las fuertes lluvias que también hacen las semillas germinar que durante el verano caluroso el fuego que ardió sobre la naturaleza en un ciclo más de la cosecha y prosperidad natural leyes que regulan nuestras vida vendrán cada verano e invierno hasta y el fin del tiempo y hombre viva y su mundo protegido por sí y el que así lo quiera nos dará muchas y grandes ejemplos de cómo la vida se debe tratar en el cielo y en la tierra. Pero bien en momentos de angustia y dolor en plenitud o fortuna. Y así pues cuando la naturaleza parecía dormida y hechizada por los rayos de la luna nosotros esperamos que saliera en el horizonte y en tanto no había más bueno que algo de comer para todos en la casa y asomado a la ventana desde allí buscábamos el aparecer de una hermosa y clara luna que nos pone en el trance de la noche haciendo que nuestra mente se relaje y en la paz de Dios vague por los lugares que uno más le fascinan haciendo que la entre en nosotros la paz de la noches de lunas tan apreciadas por la familia y el pueblo en fiesta permanecería hasta que amaneciera el día y llamándonos al campo donde los hombres del pueblo labran los terrenos y se dedican a las labores del día y adornando los prados siempre cuando amanecía el día se vía caminar hacia los sembrados que tanto orgullo le causo y esperando el tiempo que uno llamaba los buenos espíritus del bien para que las cosechas fueran buenas él viajaba todos los días del año hasta que personalmente el llevara su carga en los hombros y llevando hasta su casa para que todos disfrutaran de los alimentos y el orgullo del sembrador del campo. Y entonces aquí venimos todos con él para agradecer su esfuerzo y su sudor que siempre derramo sobre el suelo en honor al señor nuestro Dios que nos da la voluntad de hacernos con El al campo lleno fe y entonces así iba pasando el tiempo en ese lugar y además los hijos del sembrador crecían en el hogar para que cuando iba al campo ellos lo seguirían desde la distancia hasta los sembrados y también por el camino se notaban las flores que admirando desde lejos con ojos de amor El sembrador siempre disfrutaba y de su perfume en el silencio de la noche amaba y se demoraba su presencia en la noche de lluvia y la luna su camino alumbraba cuando él viajaba en los caminos de ese pueblo que tanto progreso al pueblo dio este sembrador que siempre se hizo notar en camino al vecindario del pueblo y sus vecindades, y así fue que con mucho esfuerzo y coraje el sembrador se fue llevado a frente de los más sobresalientes del pueblo y con gran alegría fue el uno de los más fuertes y humildes en el pueblo del sembrador y sus vecindades. Así un día después de mucho tiempo hizo su apariencia entre muchos, todos notaban su presencia de noble y fuerte hombre que además de sembrar y entre otras se dedicaba el sembrador del campo pues El así lo quiso en su mente y alma y que cuando le miraban a sus ojos se notaban las cualidades del humilde y valiente que era este sembrador que su vida dedicara al este oficio tan humilde y tan fuerte esfuerzo requería a este y cualquiera que su tiempo dedicara al buen trabajo pues para Dios es su gente su gloria y su orgullo fue inmenso e increíble y muy difícil de describir con palabras, hasta que uno realice las fuerzas que fluyen dentro de sí al voluntario y libre albedrio un día se dedicó a labrar la tierra del campo para así cumplir con el mandamiento de los labradores que son hombres de bien y de honor al Dios que le vio nacer de la naturaleza y se llenó siempre y por a siempre gran salud y coraje de hombre un día llamado por la fuerza suprema a llevar y aportar un gran mensaje a los hombres que habitan la tierra pues para El no vio más que el final del trabajo un gran porvenir de los hijos y gran valor para su persona tan humilde y gentil de su alma. Entonces para cuando su aparición se hizo presente en el pueblo los que le conocieron lo veneraron con mucho amor y paz que tan bueno hacia al sembrador del campo. Entre tanto al caer la noche y la lluvia se hacía presente en el lugar del sembrador los llantos de la naturaleza lo despertaron muchas veces para con el compartir el sentimiento del amor por uno y otro, así fue la noche pasando y los ojos mojados por la fuerte lluvia le impedían ver el camino y el sembrado pero las flores del camino le llenaban el corazón de valor y sus coraje fue tan grande y fuerte como el mismo cielo que se saturaba allá arriba en el cielo de donde mana el agua pura para sus campos regar con toda atención al sembrado y poniendo su esfuerzo El sembrador daba de comer a los hijos y amigos que en el campo de ese pueblo vivan en él. Así cuando uno cuando más piensa en El no más quiere ser su amigo para ir al campo donde sale el producto de su labor que fue su compañero por anos y entre las penumbras de las noches crecían los más codiciados poderes del sembrador que tan bueno hace al hombre de bien. Entonces cuando uno pasa por ahí no más que puede verlo en pensamiento como espíritu de amor y paz que nos da el placer de ver y sentir el labrador un día que fuera al pueblo para las fiestas celebrar en honor de los hombres que se dedican al oficio y con el trabajar con los elementales de la naturaleza y por supuesto ser un cristificado por su esfuerzo de gran valor y coraje entre todos los hombres que su vida pueden dedicar al trabajo como un ejemplo de ser, y de compasión, por el deber y sacrilegio de los que fueron humildes y mansos de corazón y valor que solo ellos lo podían soportar en el mundo del valle de los hombres que se dedican al bien ya al trabajo como devoción de honor y prosperidad para los hombres de buena voluntad. Y para entonces uno va por el camino que solía caminar el sembrador tan hermoso y callado como la noche que murmura al oído del sembrado, por tal razón uno no más debe de dar las gracias al sembrador por tal motivo de sacrificio y honradez por mucho, fue su labor y su perfecto conducir del hombre que por las noches de lluvia solía esconderse en sus penumbras para ir al sembrado y así cuidar de la tarea de cosechar la bienvenida noche de lluvia que tanto bueno hizo a los hombres de buena voluntad y fuerza de voluntad para poder realizar los trabajos del campo y así el con todo los poderes de su mente y su salud, así fue bendecido por Dios y la naturaleza por su parte el regalo el bienestar de la salud. Pero por eso decimos que los secretos de la noche son muy preciosos para todos pues cuando uno menos los espera se nos presentan los más bonitos pensamientos del espíritu divino sin temor a el sacrificio y el esfuerzo de que Él pudo hacer para mantener su vida salva y de su lado todo el terreno que tan bueno fue el producto como el mensaje de el sembrador del campo. Y desde ahora aprendimos a tratarnos con buen modales pues así fue como uno en mundo aprende a vivir con el hermano y siendo un grupo fuerte y unido no hay manera de que uno pereciera al ataque de las entidades del cuerpo de la mente donde se procesan los actos a proseguir en el futuro y entonces para que el hombre se cumplan sus sueños materiales hay que pensarlo y estar seguro de que es lo que uno quiere sin duda alguna y no habrá temor a equivocarse cuando los actos se cumplan en el físico pasando primero por nuestra mente de y la inteligencia a partir de aquí sé que le dará mucha importancia a la capacidad de pensar y ser el que una vez más se le diera la oportunidad de escoger entre el bien y el mal pues la mente humana se le ha desarrollado para que nuestra inteligencia nos de la verdadera y real causa de los hombres que han forjado los destinos de un mundo mejor y más seguro que el que nuestros antepasados tuvieron en un tiempo lejano, pero no sabiendo que al mente pudo ser como formas de proseguir hacia el futuro y sin duda a perder el tesoro de los hombres que utilizaron la mente como un instrumento de bien y no lo utilizaron consiente del daño provocado por el mal uso del cuerpo mental una vez que se halla desarrollado y en busca de conocimiento nos dirige al futuro del universo sin ningún temor a equivocarse y llevar a cabo sus actos de acuerdo con el uso de su mente y la experta certeza de la inteligencia fue con la realización los más nobles instrumentos del que un día nació en el mundo de la buena fe, pues eh, allí que uno no vive solo abemos muchos que necesaria mene se debe respetar y la vida uno se le da lo que vale como valor en sus favores para seguir el sendero del más allá sin duda de que se equivocase en pasados tiempos de angustia y sin esperanza de tener un futuro próspero y grandioso para todos los que en el confieran sus estudios y sus enseñanzas de la vida que se le fue otorgada por la divinidad y hombre que fue muy honesto y seguro de ser un ejemplo para los que aún tienen miedo de ser hombres de al menos simples y poco reconocidos proyectos durante su vida tan agobiada por los errores del pasado y a veces ya sin ninguna esperanza se llenaron egos sin permitir el paso a los mundos superiores del hombre que poco a poco trascendería los pensamientos y actos derechos y justamente la verdad y el conocimiento se diera por añadidura al que en un buen tiempo se dedicara al buen y practico ejercicio de los derechos y los deberes del individuo de dedicados al gran y magnifico propósito de llegar al sublime de su credulidad en las leyes del universo y su respeto al más grande de sus sueños el de vivir con la esperanza y respeto por las leyes del universo, a las que sus poderes se le rendían a su paso y la naturaleza lo habría de venerar a su paso por el comino a hacia el más allá, sin que uno pueda tener duda a equivocarse en un futuro o el presente también, entonces así fue que de verdad que este mundo es de los que aman a sí mismo y los demás al igual, no habrá cabida para los que quieren destruir la obra del misterio y los enseñanzas del maestro que fue en busca y en pos del paz y amor pues su cuerpo alma y espíritu se unieron en un esfuerzo por dedicarlos al bien y ser como un puente al lado apuesto del rio, y entonces así como un hombre se conoce por sus actos así es su humildad y también su poder se le dio por añadidura al paso de los años que vivo en este mundo de tanto y grandiosa fortuna y el placer de vivir en el mundo de los amigos y todos en la comunidad serán sus devociones en un futuro que tal vez será el máximo presente para todos. Y también en el interior del corazón se sentía la paz y el amor por todo pues es ser humano ama y quiere como lo hacen los verdaderos amantes que en secreto se unen con Dios adorando su pareja y deseando su buen porvenir y total alegría para todos, por eso en el pueblo se celebraban las fiestas del amor y así que el amor se manifestaba y la ley fue por siempre respetada en veneración de la suprema autoridad confiando y asegurando la fe de estar siempre de su lado para, un día no muy lejano poder ser uno más de los que con gran valor se les unieran y se le viera como el sembrador trabajando la tierra o en su hogar los oficios del diario y viviendo en un eterno ahora para que se le cumpliera su honorable y justa decisión que así se le vino a su mente cuando el empezó a realizar sus ideas vivas en un rincón de su mente especial para los sagrados y los íntimos pensamientos de su persona, a la que más tarde se diera por regalo a los que con El unidos con lazos de amor también le siguieron por los caminos de la perfección y la superación del ser como un nuevo ser que traería mucha bienaventuranza a todo el pueblo y sus vecindarios y que Él se diera un día recogido por los grandes maestros del pasado con el propósito de hacer el mundo un lugar de mucha felicidad y también pues es necesario para los hombres el oficio el más querido y preferido pasatiempos del ahora y siempre en todo el mundo. Así que cuando uno ve los trabajadores la envidia y el coraje de un niño se le deja ver en el enrojecido rostro pues para el no habrá más felicidad que la de aprender a labrar la tierra y trabajar con sus amigos del pueblo, en estos momentos cuando es muy notado el hombre se da a conocer por sus oficios y sus actividades son diarias además se ve su honra y su lealtad a la que un día se unió en el amor por ella siempre fuerte y con admiración por el vio nacer un fuerte y hermoso niño de sus amores con la amante de su vida, y un día cuando el sol salió temprano en el este su mirada se irguió junto a el árbol que sembró en el lugar que frecuentaba con ella a su lado, para entonces ya su sabiduría seria basta y la devoción por los sagrados y bencitos tesoros del pueblo una vez pronuncio su soberanía y respeto por los frutos de su amor por ella cuando su corazón y su alma dio por completo a su gran amante de todos los tiempos y en cuanto a sus hijos él quiso mucho pues ellos siempre fueron sus seguidores y fieles al derecho y el sacrificio por los demás los hizo muy muy fuertes en sus interiores ya aprendidos por sus buenas enseñanzas de su experimentada y feliz vida en el pueblo de la fiesta y la amistad de todos los que al sele unieran y le fuesen fieles a las enseñanzas que se le hicieron saber a través de Dios en secreto y el amor por la humanidad. Así que para más adelante uno se puede imaginar cuando llegaban los días de fiesta y el porvenir de ese pueblo se lo debíamos a el que puso sus frente a sudar con el caliente sol del pueblo en verano y más después el mojado invierno se le vio también en el camino que conducía a los lugares secretos donde las fiestas se celebraban en pueblo, además uno no puede imaginar la alegría del sembrador cuando la lluvia venia y su cuerpo también empapado con el aguacero se va caminando hacia casa desde el trabajo con el rostro bajo y viendo la calle que todos los días llevaba a sus vecinos a los sitios de trabajo. Un día también el vio el niño que con gran envidia deseaba ir con él al trabajo y así que como no podía por edad su envidia se le notaba en su tierno mirar y cuando pensaba en él, solo quería ser grande y fuerte como él y seguir el camino del sembrador así trazado por los que con él se le unieron en un esfuerzo por llegar a ser como El. Así pues iba el hombre con destino a su lugar preferido de los amantes de los pequeños del amor y más allá se vean en secreto y juntos llevaron a cabo los planes para un lugar de enseñanza e instrucción en donde se fuera más profundo en los misterios del aprendizaje el adiestramiento del conocimiento los misterios de la vida que cuando uno piensa y se le da a conocer el significado de la vida uno no más se llena de alegría en el corazón pues él fue el ejemplar más bueno sobre todo los tiempos habidos en el pueblo de la fiesta, y para celebrar ese día de alegría todos sin pensar en más nada que el ejemplo y el amor de todos los días por el ya vividos se le otorgo también el regalo de la maestría y la compasión por todos los que en el creyeran y su fe le pudieran encomendar sus secretos de amor, tal vez por eso fue que su amante seria alguien a quien amar y ser amado y por su fértil amor fue a llegar a ser su gran amor por el Dios que desde el cenit se le vio con el rostro mojado por el sudor del trabajo y la dedicación por su familia, aun mas fue querido en secreto por miles y en el pleno del día sus recuerdos se le hacían realidad a la luz del día. Pero un día al salir el sol entre las montañas y la atmosfera yacía saturada por la humedad de la noche fría yo encontró bajo de la montaña durmiendo hasta tarde pues como un gran espíritu se le apodero de si el sueño un gran sueño le causo levantarse tarde y entre los arboles de la montaña se cubría tranquilo pues eran ellos los altos arboles le cuidaron mientras dormía pero lo importante de todo es que este sueño era la ley suprema, y desde lo alto de las montañas bajaban para entrar en su mente y así se envolviera con el poder de los elementales que viven en la montaña ; y esos momentos su rostro parecía preocupado pero como él no hablaba con nadie y solo viajaba hacia el lugar secreto donde se encontraba con su amante, no sin antes pasar cerca de la presencia del niño al que también el apreciaba mucho y al pasar frente a él se dio cuenta de que se estaba haciendo hombre y ya no mas era un pequeño, que deseaba ser como El pero el sembrador no podía decirle nada a Él o a cualquier otro los sueños y realizaciones que este tuviese en mente, así que aun siendo niño le entro un gran coraje, el aprender a labrar los terrenos del campo como El sembrador lo hacía cada día de su vida y por allí un día de buenaventura se le hizo el gran deseo de ir con El para aprender a labrar la tierra para cultivar sus alimentos de su familia y entre tanto en un momento vio que el sembrador mientras labraba la tierra se comunicaba con la fuerza superior del mundo y sin sorpresa alguna pues solo lo hacía en su pensamiento El sembrador hubo realizar sus ideas hacia lo que él venía a su pueblo enviado por la justicia para su misión llevar a cabo tan como pudiera y a la tierra fue diciendo a cada movimiento que hiciera con su herramienta mientras trabajaba la tierra pues para el acostumbrado ya al ejercicio de labrar la tierra no más, que al mirar hacia abajo al terreno se sele hacia fácil su trabajo y entre tanto también se le hacía fácil el comunicarse con la jerarquía suprema para llevar a cabo su misión, la misión de que un día todos los del pueblo le dieran su respeto del grado espiritual ganado ya anteriormente con el esfuerzo y la decisión de compartir con él los estudios del espíritu y la gran ley que nos protege, nos guía y nos acompaña hasta el rincón más abandonado del planeta, así que con este él fue al campo con el deseo de poder ser como el sembrador que tanto admiraba pues era muy respetuoso y gentil el sembrador hasta que un día cualquiera este niño que tenía tanta ansia de aprender se hizo solo al campo de donde el vio el sembrador frecuentar solo con el espíritu de la mañana cálida por el sol saliendo de las altas montañas. Así que fue magnifico el empiezo del niño que se le hizo a trabajar con herramienta y especialmente sus anhelos de ser como el sembrador algún día sin más ni menos que con las ganas ser un futuro labrador de la tierra como lo hacía el sembrador más famoso del pueblo ya para entonces alguien que puso la energía en labrar la tierra y ser el ejemplo del niño que con su celosa mirada se hiera tras de una mañana de sol. Sin darse cuenta ya el niño fue poco a poco creciendo y su mirada aun le decía que la admiración por él no era en vano pues sus ejemplos de hombre le revelaron muchas cosas sobre de la vida, más aun se dio entre si el valor y la admiración por El y sin duda se hizo hombre guiado por el sembrador y su estilo de vida fue para este niño el camino hacia el futuro y la oportunidad de llegar a ser un buen sembrador como el que caminaba todas las mañanas hacia el sembrado y le gustaba la soledad por sus enseñanzas y su orientación natural en un mundo de mucha actividad. Ahora que ya el tiempo paso y sin ningún cambio de la mentalidad del hombre que fue a llegar y ser el que guardaba los secretos del corazón pues es lo que primeramente se reflejó en el hombre que a su paso camino al encuentro con la verdad y la perfección mental acordándose de los muchos casos del pasado que para todos era sus escuelas vividas en el tiempo donde uno guarda todo la información y abastece el sistema del individuo con todo su pasado informando de la actividad de un pasado en donde nadie lo vive excepto el mismo que se le dio la vida cuando el tiempo vio nacer el pequeño con propósitos de superar las técnicas de vida, así es que el tiempo y la vida van y nacen juntos y a su cuerpo penetro cuando el niño nació y se dio cuenta de que se había ya iniciado su grandiosa y afortunada vida de ese a quien veremos más adelante erguirse y dar los primeros pasos de su existencia en el mundo físico y vino del amante que vio con admiración y jubilo al ella en lugar del encuentro con Él y para que fuese aún más fuerte su hombre dio a luz a su hijo, ahora que cuando una mujer da a luz a su hijo, se tomó el curso de un tiempo muy especial y para que sea por largo tiempo el amor de los dos perfecto y puro como el día en que nació el hijo del hombre. Así que cuando el hombre fue creado y, creció yo espero y creo que el hombre puro y sano, de tranquilo corazón quiso amar y así pues que nadie sabía que era el amor excepto cuando el vio por primera vez a su pareja, para entonces él supo que para amar el hombre necesito la esposa como punto de referencia e inmediatamente vio que para que el amor nazca se necesitan dos personas y por el estilo, así que muchas cosas se hacen entre dos individuos de el mismo género, como el como el fuego y el aire son necesarios para la combustión y se alimentan de la materia como combustible para que ¡halla luz y color, con la luz vemos las cosas y calor nos da energía para trabajar y la moción la energía necesaria para mover sus cuerpos rumbo a la casa de su amada para una vez en ella los dos amantes se unieron en un gran placer in perpetua admiración por el otro, en las penumbras cuando se ven sus, ojos alumbran como dos faros de fuego; y entonces es necesario el uno para el otro más aun cuando quiso verse a sí mismo sus ojos se posaron en esposa que amablemente le saludaba en el santo lugar y dedicándose a su oficio en la casa se le ve como pasando el único tiempo que parece vivir y viajar en él y en los quehaceres de su casa, pero pensando en espíritu y cuerpo como su real ser para vivir en su querido mundo lleno de sorpresas y sueños de mucho valor para todos con la ley suprema a su servicio es grande el poder de espíritu cuando hace su aparición en pensamientos que adornan nuestra mente tanto como uno puede imaginar las cosas en el milagroso pensar. Al tiempo que uno piensa toma lugar lo que es llamado creaciones mentales cuando son materializadas en el plano físico donde podemos estudiar sus dimensiones y características que lo componen como nueva vida al tiempo ya definido y de allí en adelante ser un nuevo miembro de la gran familia del universo, al recibir el presente de vida en el instante de nacer, y durante el proceso de existencia uno va con el tiempo por anos días hasta el fin del tiempo y atreves de muchas experiencias es como el espíritu se enriquece y cada año se nos da la oportunidad de proseguir con el resto de nuestros familiares a los que tenemos el deber de respeto y admiración pues ellos son los que han hecho los preparativos de nuestro suceso y el perpetuo amanecer de la vida son para nosotros nuestro admiración por el poder divino y nuestro guía cuando aún pequeños nos abrimos paso en el fluir de la vida y respeto y cumplimiento de nuestra existencia como los habitantes del mundo que son nuestro tesoro de por vida. En cuanto más indagan sobre del origen de mente como cuerpo de espíritu sin duda que uno puede decir que entre tanto pensamos; que es nuestro espíritu el cuerpo mental que se ha desarrollado por miles de años en ordenado proceso que enriquece la personalidad de conocimientos y descubrimiento del individuo como una figura importante en la creación de la fuerza de la voluntad y leyes gobernantes del universo y producen la armonía y el orden de la naturaleza la cual encierra los secretos de la vida y la evolución del espíritu desde el nacimiento del espíritu como el cuerpo mental y evolucionar hasta llegar a ser el hombre en existencia y también como la figura moderna y de gran habilidad para manipular la naturaleza en un ejemplo de la creación y evolución de la vida dentro y fuera de sí, dando lugar a la realización y la inteligencia y la voluntad del individuo capaz de saber entre el bien y el mal como la color y el frio grande o pequeño y entre lo oscuro y la luz, más adelante se verá el hombre envuelto en proyectos más nuevos y modernos e intento la creación tecnológica y la realización del origen una vez que alcanzara la madures como figura de poder y sacrificio desde su aparición y entonces la mente humana es la concentración de elemento ígneo en su estado de invisibilidad y es el espíritu de la creación que en un momento dado y debido a la evolución del ser llega al estado de madures con la perfección spiritual atreves del conocimiento y grado de inteligencia del individuo, por eso se dice que el espíritu al igual que el cuerpo encuentran la perfección en los estudios realizados por el mismo pues atreves de la vida y al evolución uno aprende dándole inteligencia y sabiduría y es lo que se conoce como un espíritu maduro y fuerte, al igual que su poder es igual al conocimiento acumulado en sus entrañas, dentro del alma como el hombre del futuro deberá ser un ejemplar para los demás, y comportarse como algo puro y sano y sus conocimiento avanzado lo hará más poderoso que ninguno pues son sus tesoros adquiridos durante toda su vida y de acuerdo a su inteligencia así será su poder y la maestría como uno de los mejores atributos del alma humana y son necesarias para la subsistencia en la comunidad donde vivimos como residentes de nuestra comunidad en donde aprender es necesario para sobrevivir y mantener la marcha del tiempo y la redención de la vida para algún día ser miembros activos del mundo donde trabajamos y residimos permanente. Son pues los tesoros del alma las recopilación y experiencias de la vida y la habilidad de aprender los que constituyen; el espíritu humano o también para cualquier alma existente en el mundo. Siendo el hombre ya una figura avanzada e intelecto progresivo se dice que una vive con el tiempo en el lugar de su nacimiento en donde aprendió a hacer las cosas básicas como cuidarse el su esposa sus hijos y conviviendo con los reinos de la fauna y la flora y también su necesidad de la alimentación y la vivienda fueron los primeros y más cercanos medios y necesidades que obligaron al hombre a construir sus hogares y lugares de lujo y placer por cuanto debemos atentar con el entretenimiento y la salud y el porvenir también fueron sus metas a seguir en este tiempo y en cuanto al mismo asunto espiritual que va junto con el físico y trabajan en comunidad ya sabemos que nuestro cuerpo es donde el espíritu reside y como este es poder de la voluntad ser un hombre de buenas costumbres y modales es para nosotros importante el desarrollo de las cualidades del alma se acumulan los tesoros ya antes mencionados y que positivamente los son necesarios para la vida y la vida es con los nosotros una también; y es por eso que el progreso físico y material nos llevara al triunfo tal vez en el futuro en donde se llegara el día en que se descubren los secretos de la verdadera filosofía de seres que aún viven con esperanza y lealtad a las leyes y regulaciones que nos gobiernan como habitantes del nuestro único y universal vida perpetua siempre con ánimo y el deseo de servir a la causa del despertar de la conciencia y el amanecer del nuevo día en que nosotros veremos la luz en el cielo y la creación de Dios sobre la tierra. Y para que se cumplan las profecías serán las señales que veremos cuando cada cual haya tomado el poder y la soberanía de si como una obligación en los próximos tiempos, a seguir y que se extermine las pobrezas y el dolor y transformándose en los más grandes y notados poderes del hombre del áureo florecer del mundo; ante nuestros ojos se abran las puertas del conocimiento y la verdadera filosofía del hombre ya en camino a la eternidad y la vida pura del que con su fe y el valor se nos hace aún más obvio nuestra existencia en el universo. Por el momento sigue el camino y piensa en la paz que podemos disfrutar en el silencio y el beneficio de la educación de la perseverancia de la verdad para que el mañana sea como lo ha planeado y el hombre reclame sus derechos que han poner en alto su honesta figura como el forjador de este mundo y el porvenir muy bueno a seguir con sus sueños en el áureo florecer de la vida en un futuro cercano y sin el temor de tener sus hijos a la falsa profecía del error y también la prosperidad será admirada y protegida sobre todas las cosas seguramente han de poner su esfuerzo en los cosas divinas y sagradas para todos los que siguen el sendero de la bienaventuranza y la salvación del alma y la vida sea abundante y gentil para todos los que trabajan en el despertar de la conciencia y la ayuda al que sea presa de las inmunda falsa de la mente corrupta y errónea sin el pecado y limpio de cualquier contaminación concerniente a la salvación del que sea limpio de pecado y de gran corazón para aceptar las enseñanzas del profeta que dio todo por la salvación del hambre ya amenazado por el mal y sirviente del egoísmo y la farsante palabra y mente inútil y sin ningún aspiración y fe y admiración por el divino poder que tiene el verbo en donde se encierra la verdad y el conocimiento, el intimo el que posee la vida y la gracia del espíritu santo; ojala se haga la voluntad de los puros y los seres de buena fe nos presten atención y su devoción por la causa nos llenen de alegría a los que son sanos y limpios de toda mancha de pecado y llenos del pudor del creador nos reestablezca y nos guie al amanecer del día y por mucho tiempo seamos saturados del amor y la paz de Dios. Mientras tanto El en su lecho descansa hasta el amanecer del día, con la intención de seguir las actividades en donde Él trabaja pues para un hombre es importante ejercer el oficio que El así lo quisiere por su voluntad y su decisión al amanecer de la vida cuando sus ojos vieron por primera vez la madre natura y ella en si como si fuese llevando "consigo la fruta de vida siempre con ella"; en sagradas entrañas; y cada vez que veamos un nacimiento se cumplirá el gran milagro de la creación; una nueva vida empezara su trayecto en y atravesó del tiempo y cada año sea marcado con un sello de amor como recordando el día en que nació, su cumpleaños desde que fue un niño hasta su madurez donde el alcanzara muchos grados de maestría y adiestramiento para tener el control de si en control y su estado de conciencia al sumo grado de alerta porque, para un hombre es importante el y es necesario para vivir en su pueblo con el mensaje del sembrador que así fue como el hombre que tiene la soberanía del grupo y hace crecer el alimento de sus hijos, cuando llega el momento de regresar al trabajo desde el corazón sale al voz del amor por su familia, siguiendo el ejemplo de los maestros y forjadores del amanecer de la vida y más; por eso cuando al amanecer uno ve el labriego dirigirse al campo para que sus cultivos sean buenos y alimenticios a todos; y entonces al igual que el hombre que se dedicó a recorrer el mar en su embarcación se hizo al mar y entre tormenta y buen tiempo pudo sus redes llenar de una caza de muy buen tamaño y para este su embarcación fue su morado por todo el tiempo que este estuvo en las agua del mar. Así pues se marcan la vida de todo hombre con el tiempo que nunca se detiene y por su supuesto es parte de si su vida dura en tanto el tiempo marche y marche en un intenso y dulce amor que nos ha de dar el pase al próximo ano el de mucho y saturado del por su gloria como la niebla en las montañas se nos presenta ante y justamente en nuestro frente para gran asombro del pequeño que poco a poco camina hacia ningún lugar en especial y siguiendo a sus padres él va a lugares donde se reúnen la gente para hacer celebraciones y compartir las fiestas del frutal de donde saldrá el sustento de todo un gran tesoro con orgullo para sus esposa e hijos que siempre cada mañana el hijo vio partir muchas veces al campo con la esperanza de ir con él al campo donde se labra la tierra y el fruto de su trabajo nace cado año gracias al sembrador del campo que muy fuerte pero humilde también trabajo en el campo labrando sus mejores terrenos del pueblo; ayudando a la ecología también dando lujo a la madre natura al mismo tiempo con su hermosos "frutos vivo en la madre" de amor y paz. Ahora encargado de los asuntos aquí en lo personal y lo privado el asunto de lo inmundo y la fuerza divina o diríamos las fuerzas del bien y del mal ; latentes en todo cuerpo viviente y son estas las encargados de la balanza de del karma y el darma, la que son el sí mismo son lo que uno es, son exactamente satán y Dios en pleno balance lo que es bueno y nos hace fuertes como los invencibles del intimo que mora en y es uno mismo al igual; entonces cuando el hombre trabaja sobre si, sobre la personalidad y las habilidades de desenvolvimiento único de lo que existe es la vida en sí y aquí decimos la vida y la muerte pues bien ellas existen en nosotros son el mí mismo y ahora tenemos que poner el ejemplo del trabajador que cuando trabaja la tierra y recoge las cosechas para alimentar su familia y formar su hogar en el lugar donde este se estableciera por supuesto algunos decimos que para que el trabajo; pues bien explicaremos por qué el laborar es por supuesto nuestro sustento y nuestro seguro de vida, pues ya sabemos que le pasa al que no trabaja y no le interesa el laborar y la superación personal del individuo, y para que la superación se lleve a cabo sabemos tenido que pasar ciertas prácticas de conocimiento y aprendizaje, y llevándose a cabo sobre la filosofía y la creencia de que uno vive en este mundo para aprender y superarse durante el ciclo de vida porque nadie le podrá hacer el trabajo por él, es más allí se quedara estancado el hombre que no laboro en la causa del aprendizaje y la superación personal del mismo y ahora hablando de estas cosas tendremos que ver el tema de que las fuerzas del bien y las fuerzas del mal son como los paralelos existente en y dentro de si para entonces ya habremos reconocido las fuerzas, las dos que van una a la par de la otra son las que hacen posible el supera miento de individuo llevándolo al triunfo al destino de su jornada que se nos ha designado en el transcurso y el inicio de nuestra vida cuando apenas éramos niños ; se han presentado ante nuestra presencia el dilema del ser o no ser que los profetas hablan en sus escritos, son estos los que han dedicado su preciosa vida al sacrificio por sus hermanos hombres de bien, de buena voluntad que trabajan en busca de las respuestas y los secretos que la naturaleza encierra en sus entrañas dentro de las dimensiones de la verdad y la farsa y es la vida en si en donde uno debe aprender a vivir con el resto de los otros hombres que pueblan la tierra. Para mi estas fuerzas del bien y del mal existen en mí, son las entidades que componen la persona son las fuerzas del bien y del mal las que en un momento dado nos llaman para que se cumplan las leyes del universo son las reglas del universo las que uno trabaja siempre día y noche durante mucho tiempo en nuestras vidas nos hacen fuertes o nos hacen débiles nos entrenan y nos para la lucha real con nosotros una vez alcanzada la edad de elegir durante el aprendizaje en que uno tiene que escoger entre el bien y el mal entre las fuerzas de lo divino a las fuerzas del mal; pero aquí hay que decir que trabajando con si mismo solo una debemos servir pues eh ahí que si uno escoge el mal en el lugar del bien perecerá entre la maleza y el desafortunado lapso que este duraría mientras se dedica a la andanzas del hombre que no aprendió a vivir con las fuerzas del bien y del mal; son pues ellas las que un hombre superdotado habrá de estudiar y reconocer entre el bien o el mal ente la vida y la muerte solo los que han trascendido el lapso del principiante para luego pasar a los estudios del gran iniciado entre los misterios mayores que se le fueron dados en el transcurso del vivir y debido al aprendizaje en su vida ha de llegar a su completo desarrollo y poder de control sobre si, pues en estas situaciones habrá un balance entre las fuerzas del bien y del mal y estas últimas se hicieron el campo de batalla y el campo de entrenamiento para el soldado que pretendiera ganar las batallas de la sobrevivencia y pasar al gran y poderoso estado de cristificado y transformado habiendo entonces vencido la muerte y pasar a mas ocultos lugares donde morar por los siglos y tener la recompensa de transformar las fuerzas del mal en fuerzas útiles para el aprendizaje y para tener la gran dicha de ser el vencedor de la batalla entre el ser y el no ser promulgado por los grandes que maestros de la logia ya transformados y consientes del gran esfuerzo por estos durante su vida; un gran ejemplo para los que vienen detrás con la incógnita del ser o el no ser de la filosofía secreta de los hombres que valerosamente llevaron a cabo en el transcurso del tiempo no muy lejano. Entonces aquí diremos que la vida en un principio siempre habrá el riesgo de no poder pasar al más allá donde uno encontrara toda clase de tesoros del alma y el espíritu se saturaría de ese amor y la sabiduría del maestro que nació al vencer los obstáculos del sendero que conduce a la vida eterna, el bienestar de la vida segura y gentil del hombre que hubo logrado la cima de la montaña y la fortuna de haber vencido el mal transformando estas fuerzas en algo muy útiles para el hombre que las tiene encarnadas dentro de sí pues estas fuerzas no fueron ya una amenaza para el, más bien el al transformo en algo muy sagrado y útil para e hombre de poder y gloria sobre la naturaleza y entonces debemos decir que cuando cada uno de nosotros al principio de la vida habrá caminar con cautela pues eh ahí que si deliberadamente se proclama y se dedica a las practicas malas del mundo y ya sabiendo la diferencia del mal y el bien, las consecuencias de la mala conducta pasaría al proceso de su desaparición sobre de la faz de la tierra pues no podrá seguir el paso de los demás y tendrá que ser dejado atrás a la intemperie donde la tormenta probablemente causara su muerte y su desgracia pues no habrá quien lo pueda ayudar pues en esta vida hemos sido creados a imagen y semejanza del uno con el otro sin ninguna diferencia es de uno la vida, le pertenece y es el único que se le presentan las oportunidad ser un trabajador de conciencia y capaz de manipular los elementos en sí, ya que cuando él nació su vida fue cometida a la escogencia entre el bien y el mal cosa que uno debe hacer la vida su gran mundo de paz y convivencia y pues es algo de acuerdo con las leyes que gobiernan el universo y más aún el hombre; la más exaltada figura del mundo y al día saldrán las señales de un mundo lleno de grandeza y prosperidad por eso les digo que cuando es uno un niño se le presentaran las escogencias a seguir en la vida futura llena de incógnitas y ahí nosotros tenemos que hacer las escogencias a seguir hacia el futuro hacia la vida o hacia la muerte en donde no más se hallara un mundo sin poder ni grandeza pues su persona no estudio ni se superó y es más se llenaría de defectos y entidades que le impedirán el avance en el sendero de la vida que conduce a la bienaventuranza de quien así lo quiera y su decisión es un pacto con el mundo un gran paso a la vida eterna atreves de miles de noches y días productivos que aprovechamos en y durante la vida en posesión por el individuo siendo el libre albedrio su camino a seguir con la voluntad de llegar a ser alguien a quien el mismo se sorprendiera con todo fervor y el amor de la naturaleza se abrirá paso ante si por su buena conducta y su extraordinario poder que le serviría para su beneficio íntimo. Ahora viniendo la paz sobre la tierra nosotros somos los único dueños de la vida los que van a ser el ejemplo a todos los que vendrán detrás y le seguirán sus pasos hasta donde el comino se lo llevara en un tiempo de felicidad y armonía siendo su obediencia a las leyes de los humildes de corazón y su sabiduría sus tesoros del espíritu. Los que en tiempo se pudieron transformar en las armas para conseguir las metas de los estados mentales que uno de proponga con el poder de la voluntad uno podría alcanzar estas metas tomándolas por sorpresa en trabajo sobre sí mismo en un esfuerzo por mantener la conciencia alerta y la mente bajo control pues es ahí, una vez más, donde residen las fuerzas del bien y del mal haciéndola uno de los centros donde se procesan las ideas y las percepciones de nuestra vida, pero no es también el resto de los centros importantes y de buena observación el cuidarse cuando se usan eso también incluye ser el comandante de su propia vida, hoy día tendremos que con los avances en el estudio y cambios en sistema como para aseverar que hoy se ha alcanzado la cima de la sabiduría como para explicarla en simples palabras que sean entendidas por todos. Así que cuando decimos que la voluntad hace un hombre lo que es; nos referimos al destino a tomar durante su vida y siendo uno inteligente por naturaleza más aún tenemos que hacer buenas decisiones hablando sobre el destino y las metas del futuro sean trazadas en vida del individuo pues cuando es demasiado tarde no abra tiquete de regreso será un viaje sin regreso, pero hay también el hombre que escoge por voluntad el camino del bien tendremos que decir que, son los afortunados de la vida pues uno estando en vida se compromete a residir y permanecer en el planeta, y para su sorpresa y tentación de muchos hay que voluntariamente haga la decisión de vivir como quiera a su propia voluntad entonces creeríamos que sería fácil y divertido el infringir la ley sin que uno sea penado por las mismas leyes, pues ya estuvo dicho que lo que uno quiere es lo que se hace lo que le plazca en nuestra corta vida, y entonces uno dice que quera disfrutar de la vida y practicar los hábitos del mal y como hay oportunidad de cometerlos, pero no quiere decir; tendremos la vida libre de albedrio o libre de toda ley y quebrar sus principio de respeto y las leyes que desarrollo nuestro universo no serán quebrantadas sin el debido procedimiento a seguir cuando es llamado al tribunal para dar cuenta de sus actos, y entonces una vez expuestos los asuntos a seguir se hará justicia en la tierra pues si una vez se quebrantó la ley seguidamente no habrá cabida a la buena conducta y se convertirá en un delito grave al que la ley no pondrá ninguna atención pues es cierto que la ley no protege los que se declaran enemigos contra la ley al quebrantarla se le cerraran las puertas al comino de la un áureo florecer de la vida y el resto será cuestión de un final muy desafortunado cuando se enfrenta el individuo a los cargos ya mencionados, entonces tenemos que los pecados falsos y los falsos argumentos son las mismas tentaciones del ser interno dirigidos a los mundos bajos y de poca percepción hacia lo que realmente la vida es en su original concepción dirigida hacia el bien y no el mal; así llamamos los acciones del hombre para consigo y para con los demás también, entonces tenemos que uno que no trabajara ni para el mismo debería tener en cuenta que las leyes se hicieron con la intención de poner el orden y al paz entre los hombres y entonces el que no quiere, las leyes respetar seria perdido por el mismo, en una lucha por mantener su vida en actividad, por eso muchos años pasaron sin que hubiese paz en la tierra sin descanso alguno hubieron negociaciones hasta que se dieron las oportunidades y lugares donde residir después de la muerte, ya que sin el amor ni la compasión y las buenas actos del hombre se dará cabida a el mal, el que crecería enorme y torpe hasta llegar la degeneración del individuo mental y corporalmente corroído ya no podrá funcionar normalmente debido a que una vez más él se alejó del bien y sirvió al mal en su lugar, sin siguiera saber que era ni de dónde venía, sin saber a dónde lo llevarían cuando cometía los actos de indigna y de valor bajos, como se decía antes el que se dedica a los placeres del mundo no es consciente de sus actos poniendo en peligro su seguridad como hombre de bien e inclinando la balanza contra sí, se ira desvaneciendo hasta sus centros todos corruptos y sin vida y cada día que pasaba más el tiempo sin fin ni principio y para hacerlo renovar el lapso de vida una vez más se nos hace imposible y será revocado porque al paso de los anos la pobreza y la miseria lo devastaron con el poder de la espada y el poder del fuego lo cegó para siempre. Es más aún muchos quizás algún día retrocederá hacia donde proviene con una mente dañada y de torpe pensar en un mundo de soledad y frio como el hielo. De cualquier manera uno puede seguir adelante con su personalidad, que a propósito se forma en su infancia con las experiencias que van tomando solidas fundaciones en la mente fuertes suficientes como para seguir luchando en la lucha por conquistar su mundo por venir, una mente sana y fuerte puede entender muchas cosas que diariamente suceden en el tiempo presente puede saber cuáles son los elementos positivos de los negativos así como se dará cuenta de la verdad al conversar con alguien se le revelaran los secretos de una sencilla charla en pleno desarrollo que pasa durante su vida en cualquier situación que pueda interesarle a la persona como ejemplo de inteligencia y comprensión mental, ahora que penetramos en el campo del intelectualismo humano es como vemos que unos se ven interesados por diferentes cosas y las situaciones que el hombre como hombre tiene que solucionar si quiere ser un hombre completo deberá también ser capaz de tener un cuerpo de voluntad listo para hacer cosas que son primordiales en la vida como son el caminar y otras pues como vemos el niño cuando nace no puede hacer las cosas a su voluntad el dependerá de la madre para sobrevivir en cualquier campo de desarrollo personal como son por ejemplo comer dormir caminar preparar los propios alimentos y hasta sembrar las cultivos que le servirán para su convivencia en la vida y aquí tenemos que somos seres que crecen se desarrollan llegan a la edad adulta y sus conocimientos serán usados como una herramienta para el hombre que se dedica al trabajo de labrador el por ejemplo se verá obligado a poner en práctica sus conocimientos y experiencia a su servicio para que él pueda salir avante en el desarrollo de sus habilidades como labrador del terreno donde el crecerá las cosechas que alimentaran sus familias para empezar a su vida como adulto y sobreviviente de las leyes que gobiernan los estados naturales de la vida en cualquier sitio que uno viva y durante su etapa de aprendizaje él ha de esforzarse hasta el máximo de sus habilidades para ser el sobreviviente de los que verán las diferentes formas de vida naturales más sorprendentes nunca antes vistas por el hombre y sus familia. Interesantemente podemos poner unos ejemplos de la vida real y es así que se dan casos de alumnos que no quieren aprender las lecciones del maestro y perderán el tiempo en cosa que no son importantes y sus vidas serán un desecho y no aprenderán nada y se perderán en sus vanos pensamientos a la deriva son personas sin futuro y se verán obligados por sus hechos a seguir la vida sin ningún propósito para más luego perderse en la vejez y sin ayuda para seguir subsistiendo como hombre morirá hasta que nadie se acordara de sus características que lo reconocían como miembros de su comunidad un día joven y fuerte con la juventud en su rostro y no supo aprovechar el don del pensamiento o la capacidad de aprendizaje dedicado solamente al vano y temporal mundo de la fantasía donde encontrara un mundo vacío y el precipicio de la mente ignorante y torpe sin ningún propósito en la vida; un vano tiempo en el planeta.

Entre las penumbras como una sombra caminaba lento y ya agotado y adolorido por el frio pensaba de cuan felices fuese el mundo si nosotros nos hubiésemos comportado de manera más adecuada al tiempo de nuestros días ya agobiados por el tiempo y la vida llena de conflictos y temores de muerte que por allí disque no nos vamos a corregir del modo de ser, pero bien y en cuanto avanzaba por el sendero que parecía no ir a ningún lugar de mi destino pues ya en mi cansada mente el más feo sentimiento en mi espalda como la fría muerte me acompañaba en la fría montaña y por el sendero me atormentaba mientras caminaba por el sendero del destino, y sin mucho que esperar el hombre que yo creía saber era muy posible de caer en el sendero de la vereda que no conducía a ningún lugar pues la niebla y el viento era mis peores enemigos en ese momento de angustia que sentía en mi alma ya sin esperanzas de sobrevivir en camino al destino que nunca se cumpliría y sin ningún tiempo que pudiere perder pues era preciso el llegar al destino antes de caer agotado en el sendero y la penumbra de los fríos que me entraban en el alma como lanza de hierro sin piedad y el dolor de la mis ya agrietadas manos se me hincharon de modo que no podía sentirme sin el dolor que poco a poco me vencía en el sendero sin destino y los pensamientos eran más y más oscuros y sin vida pues el frio de la montaña me impedía seguir adelante pues era ya demasiado tarde para retroceder en busca de auxilio y ya nadie podría oír el llanto de amargura que por ahí me torturaba el interno de mi ser pues ni eso podía ya pelear contra el frio de la montaña y entonces para más desgracia iba ya mi vida un tanto descontrolada por el intenso y la fuerza del frio de la montaña me vencía sin piedad de la verdad es que ni el tiempo ya se notaba aun cuando había un rayo de luz en frente del sendero del destino. Así fue que cuando avanzaba al despertar del día mis ojos llorosos por el frio no alcazaba a ver el segundo paso de nuestro sendero hacia el destino de lo que no sabía dónde aun llevaría el sendero de la vida y la muerte también. Sim ningún sentimiento de piedad el viento se apoderaba de espalda como una sombra del tempano y para que nosotros los que empezamos el viaje sin regreso sin un destino seguro era imposible de descifrar el primer motivo de la jornada. Por eso y sin un momento que perder le implore al Dios de la montaña un favor, el de aliviar el dolor del alma que agobiada por el castigo ya no respondía al mandato de la mente ya también gastada y sin fuerzas de seguir en el sendero oscuro y frio de la montaña, pero bien no era el gigante de la mañana la que estaba en mi contra era el amor por él lo que me mantenía en movimiento para de pie, seguir el camino de mi destino que más adelante me hizo el maestro de las tinieblas y la vista del águila que por encima en las nubes y las tinieblas me querían dirigir al destino de la jornada pues para nosotros el único y verdadero sentimiento bueno y seguro de seguir es el amor y la justicia del Dios que nos acompañó en el sendero de las tinieblas que conducen al lugar de donde el sol es radiante y pacido y cálido como la leche que mana de los ríos de la naturaleza y él nos da la salud cuerpo que nos provee un lugar donde llegar y donde vivir en unión de los todos los sentimientos de las delicias del hogar y de los ríos y la luz del cálido sol nos da la vida eterna y nos da salvación por el mas fabuloso y hermoso también que es como la miel, un gran rio de miel en donde bajan las criaturas del bosque para del alimentar sus hermosos y bellos cuerpos donde sus almas viven con el único y primer sentimiento el de ser como Dios nos ha mandado ser pues es para nosotros el gran valle de la delicias y el paraíso de donde los ríos manan leche y miel.

Ahora que viene a mí el deseo de compartir los sentimientos de amistad y por mucho tiempo en silencio los secretos nos invitan a compartir con los demás la alegría de una vez haber hallado el amor y la realización de nuestro ser, un día con mucho esfuerzo llevaba sobre sus hombros el peso de la labor ya encomendada por la logia y con los deseos de que nosotros nos cubriera nuestro señor con las bendiciones del infinito mundo del pensamiento y el amor ya una vez empezado por el Cristo que nos enseñó el camino a la salvación del hombre como un gran problema para el avance delos estudios y la evolución del mundo y proseguir por las sendas del gnosticismo y el aprender los diferentes métodos de vida, pues para uno la satisfacción del encontrar el camino a la salvación y el estudio de los diferentes asuntos que ciertamente nos conciernen a todo ser humano para progresar en el camino de la salvación. Pues eh allí que nosotros estábamos interrumpiendo el avance de la evolución del universo y con mucha razón pues el hombre sufría de los más extraños y duros males, sin notar él porque del dolor humano, y es exacto porque tubo educación, la desdicha callo sobre el como una maldición que lo siguió a todo lugar, pero Dios tuvo piedad del hombre y envió ayuda para su confort y su bienestar. A este tiempo hemos alcanzado la cima de la montaña y hemos logrado despertar al nuevo y áureo florecer de la nueva era y el conocimiento ha sido capturado en nuestras mentes en buena hora y para bien de todos, alcanzando el grado de maestría en los asuntos de cualquier rama de conocimiento ya sea religioso o científico o moral, así hoy nos regocijamos por avances y la tecnología se da por reconocida en el mundo desde que no hay bases para respaldar las teorías y prácticas en esta rama de avance tan sorprendente y fenomenal como lo es en el siglo XX y desde ahora en adelante se le dará suma importancia a las ramas tecnológicas el merecido lugar en los campos de adelantos humanos, también hay que decir que la espiritualidad humana alcanzo un lugar de prioridad en las vidas humanas y la creación entera dándole su especifico e importante atención a la vida espiritual como un gran campo de conocimiento trascendental para el bienestar de la humanidad sin tener los problemas de raza y sexo o religión y para ahora se nos habla de muchas cosas que como hombre de razón nos proponemos salir avante pues es de suma importancia para todos los que vivimos y nos preparamos para una vida futura progresiva y abundante en todos los campos de la creación del universo y si es así todo marchara en pos de la vida con visiones al futuro con segura y exacta confidencia moral como para la sobrevivencia de los que en Dios ponen sus esperanza y de en la ley se cumplirá las profecías que tanto nos hablan estos grandes maestros de la filosofía secreta del tiempo, siendo así todo hombre tendrá la oportunidad de aprender cualquier tasca que con interés el escogiera sin temor a equivocarse ni tampoco dejar sus raíces raciales en que crecieran y hasta los rincones más remotos llegaría la enseñanza de todo tipo e interés que llamara su atención por ahí que se oirán los rumores de milagros y hechos que en el campo de la espiritualidad y ciencia se mencionara y para la cooperación ambos suficientes para su relación directa y mutuo interés. Ahora que ya hemos alcanzado la cima y la verdad ha salido a la superficie mantenernos alerta y despiertos por los egos de que nos incitan a cada momento de nuestra vida nos encontraremos alerta a cada pensamiento y deseos que no tengan cabida en nuestra existencia para pertenecer a la populación del siglo XX en momentos de alegría y sin engaño que penetrara las mentes en mutuo acuerdo y positivo disposición para que nos sea grantificada la salvación del espíritu y claro nuestro templo de residencia ganando la salvación en nuestro magnifico mundo de mil maravillas como hermanos y familia compartiremos del cielo de nuestro mundo. Así pues iremos al encuentro con nosotros mismos los hermanos de la filosofía nos harán más y más liviano el peso de la tarea que un día nos dimos al inicio de la era por pasar, sin saber el resultado de los esfuerzos y sacrificio entre todos los seres humanos y la madre naturaleza también somos entonces llamados al encuentro con los hermanos mayores de la filosofía secreta y la bella practica de los sentidos se volvieron un verdadero arte mental y usando las destrezas más finas se dedican a la labor de todo campo de investigación que nos ayude a mantener nuestro espíritu siempre dispuesto para cualquier tasca que saliera a flote en el presente tiempo sin temor a error, así pues con mucho fervor y cariño se nos dan los derechos de actuar con mucha libertad y autoridad completa sobre los campos de estudio mental espiritual y físico que proviene del mas allá de donde todo hombre quiere venir; del universo virgen y veneros o al que nosotros debemos nuestras vidas y la voluntad nos ha de llenar de orgullo por toda creación sobre la tierra. Y ahora que hemos entrado en los temas del hombre y el moderno y grandioso despertar al mundo de la naturaleza y sus repentinos fenómenos en momento dado se nos viene a la mente muchas preguntas en que vemos relacionados asuntos con el progreso de la civilización moderna y el pasado, pues debemos estudiar también esas que en pasado florecieron en la tierra y desaparecieron también; así que cuando el tiempo se manifiesta en nuestras vidas habrá de generar un progreso espiritual, moral y físicamente relacionados íntimamente, debe haber una evolución interna de la nosotros podamos sacar provecho para la vida futura en el planeta, y esa será la bases de nuestras producciones al ritmo del tiempo que hemos vivido en nuestro planeta y entonces es cuando apenas surge y la civilización entre una atmosfera saturada por el misticismo y la dedición a los mundos internos del espíritu y alcanzando la madures natural entre un áureo florecer de la moderna civilización nos inunda con tanto fervor y dedicación por el progreso de la misma y cuando amanece el nuevo día ilumina la mente con la luz natural cálida y fresca como la suave lluvia también, entonces entre la penumbra viene la creación de un mundo lleno de gracia y amor dotado de la inspiración que proviene del mas allá de lo profundo del cosmos donde moran todos los fenómenos y mecanismos que hacen el mundo marchar sin temor a equivocarse y por lo contrario satisfacción personal y también ser el primer ser en que ha puesto la mente y el físico a trabajar en pleno y mutuo acuerdo, nuestro espíritu con tanto destres y tan entrenado para calcular y diseñar los mecanismos más eficientes de la era moderna en que nosotros luchamos por formar y desarrollar métodos prácticos y saludables del momento. Así que en este momento todo va como los intento el hombre de la edad pasada en el amanecer de la civilización humana primera y virgen sabiendo que algo podía suceder o más bien esto generaría un gran adelanto en el progresivo y avanzado de la civilización moderna para llegar a conquistar ambos mundos físico e interno con dedicación y destreza para alcanzar a conquista del universo y posteriormente alcanzar grados de sabiduría tan avanzados y diseñar los tipos de vida para el futuro. Y aquí por ejemplo, hoy nos vemos con más noble e interesante proyecto de alcanzar el máximo grado tecnológico del siglo pues aquí tenemos que las maquinas nos han dado su efecto positivo en todo los campos de la tecnología, siendo así que el trabajo se nos hará fácil y placentero y la vida en general será progresiva, pues es importante para todos vivir con la comodidad al día, entonces vemos que la sociedad ha avanzado mucho en el campo de la agricultura al igual los establecimientos han alcanzado casi el máximo grado de perfección, en todo caso la sociedad avanza con el pasar del tiempo en acuerdo con la protección del ambiente natural, ya que la conservación de los elementos son de suma importancia para la sobrevivencia de las especias que habitan nuestro planeta al igual el problema del hombre sin metas espirituales se desvanecerá en el aire sin oportunidad del progreso pues es la mente y el espíritu una de las ramas más importantes en la época actual, para que el progreso espiritual ya que una sociedad sin valores espirituales podría fracasar en el tiempo y como todas las otras civilizaciones ya desvanecidas en el tiempo ya siendo estas las más sobresalientes tanto en el físico como el campo espiritual también, así tenemos los valores de espiritualidad de las civilizaciones del pasado eran ricas en la espiritualidad y respetuosas a la ley natural, pero la corrupción humana les alcanzo en la época del desarrollo y la llevo a su caída. Y es el individuo quien debe de estar alerta para que el progreso marche en acuerdo con los valores de los habitantes sobre el globo, para luego enfrentarse al realismo de la vida y con los valores del espíritu vienen a imponer las consecuencias a los hechos durante el tiempo que hubo y se presentó la vida de la civilización moderna o pasada al igual, así que tenemos que uno nace crece y viene a progresar con los valores del espíritu a su lado sin ninguna posibilidad de contaminación y entonces se lleve a cabo la pureza para el progreso del individuo que ha de presentar sus actos ante la ley natural para que en el tiempo de actuar de acuerdo con el progreso natural se cumplan las leyes y encaminar el curso de la vida al más allá y entonces la mentalidad del hombre se proyecte al futuro sin temor a equivocarse y seguro de si ellos se dan a el trabajo del despertar de la conciencia y el desarrollo de los poderes del hombre sobre la naturaleza y encausarlos al futuro de donde todo hombre sueña llegar y es de ese modo el lugar de donde proviene del corazón del universo, luz del universo y el espíritu viviría sin problema alguno sin que los elementos y el tiempo lo sometan a las leyes de la evolución natural como ya paso con el mundo pasado con el nacimiento de la civilizaciones del pasado. Al mismo tiempo aquí y en este tiempo recordamos los pasajes de la vida pasada como un sueño grandioso y desde la ventana del muestro dormitorio vemos los pasajes de la mente en secreto y saliendo la ventana como sale el sol entre las montañas vemos las imágenes moverse como un lento y hermoso panorama y lo disfrutamos como lo hace el niño cuando sale de su casa hacia el bosque donde habla en lenguas los secretos que retiene en su tierna mente y los comparte con la madre divina y el resto de los amigos también pues es para nosotros algo secreto ver las memorias salir de su lecho donde dormía y sus imágenes se volvían realidad por aquello del tiempo presente y viviendo el pasado como el mundo perdido y que nunca más volverá excepto en nuestra mente viva y llegar hasta el éxtasis de la realidad reviviéndolo cada vez que los recuerdos vengan a la mente. Así pues la naturaleza humana ha sido muy sofisticada, la mente fue nuestro más o uno de los más perfectos centros de nuestro ser al igual nuestro que el corazón humano y el centro sexual están en continuo y directo intercomunicados entre sí para que más tarde nos hallemos con un simple y muy bien formado sistema casi perfecto y de valioso precio, pues somos entre la creación el centro de todos los demás y los que más popularidad han tenido en el presente y hasta ahora y casi fracasando por del sí mismo pues hay mucho que contar acerca de la creación del hombre como figura importante del pasado presente y futuro, con esto nosotros vemos a muchos individuos en la historia y toda la raza humana sometida al castigo del sufrimiento y por cual Dios ha puesto su mirada a la situación del estado de la humanidad y su historia lo dice todo, vemos por ejemplo Jesús el Cristo dando a conocer la doctrina del padre y demás, pues también como otro persona igual a nosotros fue sometido a sacrificar su entidad en cambio de la salud y el bien del hombre, para entonces ya nosotros en el presente siglo xx somos los que ya fuimos en el pasado, la historia se repite a medida que la gran rueda del tiempo se hace girar pues es el tiempo el encargado de renovar las vidas cada vez que hay un giro esta será renovada o denegada por sí y entonces se llevara pues si así es al tribunal de justicia en donde la balanza de la justicia decidiría la continuación de la vida. Así que a medida que aniversario del nacimiento llega a producirse también nuestros espíritu al igual que el cuerpo se gana el pasaje al más allá donde moraría por la eternidad sin ningún problema y sufrimiento y de dolor físico. Pero para mientras tanto las oportunidades incontables se le presentan a nosotros una y otra vez para ser así testigos de la creación y el desarrollo y evolución del universo tenga lugar y la creación tenga el merecido lugar que merecemos. Así que una vez más nos encontramos frente al ir y venir del tiempo y apresuradamente nos dirigimos al lugar donde todos los seres han de provenir, el espíritu donde toda alma proviene es el cosmos, nuestro espíritu que tiene que ver con los centros del hombre en su constitución los que van a llevarnos al triunfo de la vida y sin duda una de las más avanzadas creaturas del universo es El y su presencia en el físico, el mundo de la creación en donde uno encontrara todos los frutos y toda clase de vida para su sobrevivencia. Es así que el que se descubre a sí mismo y lleva a cabo la resurrección y al pasión de la vida encontrara su lugar en el universo que vive día a día en marcha siempre hasta ahora en orden perpetuo sin detener su paso y la majestad de la vida donde el espíritu vive es la majestuosa relación entre el físico y la mente la relación del centro genético con nuestras vidas es importante ante todo para una relación de fuertes lasos entre la naturaleza y el hombre.

Y entre tonto nosotros caminamos el sendero de vida trazado por los profetas del pasado sin que tengamos problema con los demás pues eh ahí que también nuestras mentes tienen sus desacuerdos y se nos hacen disturbios en el pensamiento debido a su uso inapropiado en que se ven envueltos los demás centros al igual y cuando hay mal funcionamiento de los centros nos causa el fracaso al más allá de donde toda vida proviene del espíritu que está latente en nosotros y nos da vida pues el hombre es espíritu y usa su pensamiento a cada instante de su vida sin parar pues fuego que no se apaga el fuego del pensar y el espíritu que vive en nosotros pues así lo escogimos en día como todos y fuimos hombres que nos formamos del espíritu también. Y la evolución mental del hombre se aprecia cuando sus conocimientos se ven claros y el los reconoce como su posesión en el plano mental de su individualidad y persona humana pues sabemos que un hombre se reconoce por su pensamientos guardado en su interior como sus tesoros espirituales para su uso e interacción con los hermanos del alma que un día se nos han de unir al progreso de los que aún les importa un poco la vida como la única manera de llegar al triunfo de los elementos naturales y el cosmos en general como sus fronteras de destino y su más exitoso deseo de llegar a conquistarlo, en un pequeño pensamiento como lo hacen los maestros de la ley de Dios como simples personajes de la historia y evolución del hombre que han dado lucha a la muerte por su sobrevivencia y estadía en el mundo de físicamente hablando un obra de arte y el placer de sus cercano a la perfección de, y por su individual prosperity de su vida en su mejor y más época de adelantado desarrollo en historia del universo. Y por ahora el hombre solo espera sus tiempos de bienvenida a la edad de infinito y grande emoción del que un día fue no más que un pequeño y vulnerable hijo que poco a poco se abrió paso entre tanto engaño y difíciles situaciones del pasado y presente pues eh allí que aun y ante los ojos de los hombres la verdad se hace un hecho en todos los campos de la ciencia y al igual que la religión hoy se ha propuesto su interés en el descubrimiento de la verdadera y autentica doctrina la única que El señor nos ha enseñado a través delos profetas del mundo y también señales del más allá que aún son ocultas para los incrédulos y que pudieran infestar la palabra de Dios y su reino que no tiene ni principio ni fin lo que se conoce como uno de los misterios más y más ocultos y difíciles de explicar con palabras, pero poco a poco se nos han develado los hermanos del conocimiento y alumnos de los misterios de la vida y de la muerte como ya hemos leído en los mensajes de los maestros de los misterios mayores del conocimiento del siglo xx en un intento por recobrar el casi extinguido ser humano de los pasados ya perdidos valores de los humanos que en el mundo nos han dado un profundo dolor y entonces se ve los rumores de que hombres de mucha cultura nos han de dar a conocer el verdadero y único camino al más allá, entonces para nosotros los que aún no vemos la luz del día nos hacemos al campo de batalla con un gran sueño el de estar consiente de toda actividad que fluya en nuestro ser y sus efectos influya e inspire la conciencia para que despierte nuestro ser y seamos los salvados del señor que nos ha dado la doctrina a seguir en el futuro y desde luego ganar el terreno en camino al destino que nosotros hemos trazado cuando desde nuestra infancia cuando aun el alma no conocía el pecado y la corrupción que no dan nada más que el dolor y la ignorancia del que no quiso ver lo que estaba ante sus ojos. Por eso cuando un hombre llega al estado de pureza incondicional y voluntaria se convierte en un poder de mucho valor y Él lo utilizara para su propio y personal uso pues eh ahí que cuando se halle en el su persona se elevara a mucho más grado sabiduría y conocimiento superior y en si se sentirá como una gran energía que fluye como un gran rio en su ser, ya sabrá, que en si se halla el supremo poder del nirvana que el logro desarrollar a base de entrenamiento y trabajo interno así que cuando este humilde hombre al nacer y creciendo en conocimiento y saber se transformó en un inmortal ser supremo pues fue su esfuerzo el que lo llevo a este estado de hombre superior e inmortal habiendo pasado por los testimonios de su aprendizaje y el perfecto adelanto en su trabajo de sí mismo consiguiendo los grados necesarios para su riqueza espiritual que como material también hallo su fortuna en sí mismo y para su sorpresa fue el que con gran sorpresa su alma se llenó de la energía de los poderes y dones del alma y se ha de convertir en un maestro con poderes sobrenaturales que le darían como ya dijimos el triunfo sobre los elementos naturales y sobre su persona un total control mental y corporal incondicional que lo llevaría al triunfo de su buena y afortunada vida espiritual y pasaría a formar parte de una raza de superhombres con poderes sobrenaturales para así muy orgulloso de su familia pasaría a mas ocultos lugares y desde ese esto con la energía de las leyes del universo a su lado se convertiría en el ser supremo de jerarquía y rango que nos da la ley en si como una energía que entra en su cuerpo se hace parte de si para ir con el donde quiera que fuese y lo que hiciera le llevaría a vivir una experiencia muy agradable y con su frente al sol naciente su ser se manifestara en el de por vida. Así que ya para que un hombre llegue al estado de hombre de leyes sobre la tierra y sobre si el control perfecto y mentalidad como su espada de fuego a la que el usaría en todo momento para su estudio y para si su más precioso tesoro, pues es de mucho valor y su bien que creció en su ser desde su niñez con la ayuda de la madre que al crecer con su amor y dedicación por lo bueno y lo que el creyó en si fue suficiente para conseguir la conquista del superhombre de mucho honor y su persona no hallara más en su camino los trampas del abismo al que como ya sabemos son los campos de entrenamiento delos maestros de la ley para así un día muy pronto llegar a la cima de la montaña y desde allí poder ver el fruto de su esfuerzo que lo llevo al triunfo y la conquista de la montaña fría y sola, y al llegar a su cima recibía su precioso y delicado para su sorpresa el triunfo sobre la muerte y su inteligencia y su estado mental fue como un rayo en el cielo al descender sobre el valle que El con su trabajo cultivo muchos alimentos para su familia y sus amigos, pues para su fortuna se le dio su cuerpo y del alma como un regalo de la naturaleza desde su infancia y entonces creció entre la selva con los criaturas que fueron sus amigos desde su nacimiento. Una vez recibido el poder de los maestros y nuestro cuerpo ya saturado por la energía y el poder de la voluntad presente en Él se ve en un gran e interesante situación de la que uno no quiere dejar en un ejemplo de amor y bondad por su familia y amigos se ve atraído por el deber de compartir la enseñanza con ellos para que todos se hagan en la paz y el amor se unan en mutuo acuerdo y la lealtad de los más una vez fueron como todo los que a esta vida venimos como invitados por Dios para bajar desde el cielo con la intención de llegar a ser un ser de bien y de amor por las cosas sagradas que para bien nos han de llamar la atención e interés por lo sagrado nos llama a investigar y explorar los campos de saber de una u otra rama de estudio que nos llame la atención y los pensamientos fluyan en el cauce de la sabiduría al que uno se ve sumamente atraído por el tema y nos vemos penetrando en el interior de nuestro ser para indagar sobre de esto que nos ha llamado la atención tan intrigado por el contenido del mismo hasta entre los rincones más oscuros de la mente se vuelvan claros como la luz del día y se note los contenidos del tema y sin que llegue a tener la duda y la realización mental llegue a su máximo estado de iluminación interna y su contenido se haga claro como la luz que nos da los ojos cuando uno los abre ante el nuevo día que por milagro viene cuando el sol nos da la luz de cada día y por las noches, por las noches cuando al lecho del cálido y pacifico tiempo de descansar nos invita a soñar y nos sature de su amor. Así que en esos momentos de paz recibimos las bendiciones del ángel que nos guarda nuestros cuerpos en el lecho de amor y paz junto a la madre que nos dio tanto tanto de su tiempo y de su preocupación al ver la noche caer sobre el pueblo en que mañana aparecerá el astro solar una vez más en el oriente que nos dará pues la luz de vida y amor por todos y para todos los que en Dios creemos y nos den el pase al más allá donde se oculta y donde nace el sol, para entonces con la atención en los asuntos que nos demos a estudiar se nos hagan realidad en nuestra mente y la comprensión nos ha de inundar el ser para una vez más se nos haga los deseos y nos de los mejores frutos del campo donde se cultiva la enseñanza de los maestros y de ellos nos dé un ejemplo de admiración y el respeto por el camino a la realización del conocimiento y la paz de Dios. Por eso de acuerdo con la ley hombres de bien siempre serán humildes y porque en el mundo somos muchas clases, los que se esfuerzan por el bien y marchan en el comino del justo y el hombre que pensó en el futuro como el deber de colaborar con los demás y también con el mismo para luego disfrutar del bien en sus hogares de residencia y por las noches cuando todos duermen Él se ha de recordar el día de su nacimiento, cuando apenas era estudiante de los misterios naturales pasando primero por los aprendizajes más sencillos, luego uno ve el mundo con más prospectiva, con un puto de vista más objetivo pues ya ha aprendido a estudiar los materiales que le interesase, con el proceso de aprendizaje se le formara el carácter de hombre dedicado al espíritu y el estudio de los que hacen sus labores en tiempo pues ahí que un hombre debe saber cosas para aprender en la vida y ser el que habla con la verdad para proseguir hacia más ocultos lugares de nuestra penumbra y en cuanto sea posible tener la oportunidad de ser el que un día se ganara el nirvana y su felicidad, tomándolo por sorpresa y gran alegría pues ha desarrollado los poderes que El con gran entusiasmo quiso estudiar en un principio y cuando sus padres le crecían en la niñez y entonces se le nombro como el gran entusiasta y en si su vida le lleno de conocimiento y por supuesto su carácter fue desarrollando su personalidad definitivamente seria y concreta pues él sabe dónde su filosofía y doctrina le darían las armas de la vida para que con sus alabanzas y gloria su familia protegería de tantos peligros en camino a el nirvana y sus inesperados temas de estudio y Él se diera a la labor de su aprendizaje por voluntaria esperando ser el uno con la madre naturaleza en cuanto sea posible porque su tiempo tenía un gran valor y lo aprovecho cuando en un principio Él se dedicó a sus estudios y con la intención de ir mas allá donde el mundo se une consigo y sin tiempo que perder una vez se le presentara el oportuno y feliz ocasión de aprender la doctrina de los maestros de la ley y también de los grandes profetas que en buena hora se dedicaron a predicar las enseñanzas de todos los tiempos sin ningún interés premeditado y sin condición la enseñanza verdadera pasaría a todos los hermanos de la tierra y los grandes maestros su historias le contarían a sus hijos que con tanto amor les daría su corazón y sus tesoros más que todo espirituales se ven en sus ojos que reflejan la verdad y el conocimientos. Sabiendo el camino al cielo y el nirvana con la intención de llevar su familia por la senda de la verdad y justica pura para lo cual necesitaría indagar sobre los problemas de la humanidad y sus proyectos que el ser humano tenía que aprender al principio de la existencia cuando por la gracia de Dios y la realización de temas a que nosotros nos dieran a estudiar en vida. Así que cuando ya hubiera crecido y su tiempo a su favor en el prado por las noches se encontrara con si para compartir un momento con la soledad. Uno de los primeros maestros del esoterismo y el conocimiento nos da un gran ejemplo al compartir con nosotros los más delicados y grandiosos secretos que no dio al venir al mundo con el propósito de un día enseñar la doctrina de su padre en el cielo y en la tierra para tanto seguir sus huellas en un esfuerzo por conseguir y compartir el evangelio de los profetas de todos los tiempos. Y además sus tesoros ya mencionados su espíritu se ha de engrandecer por su bien y nos dan vida eterna y, es pues el conocimiento el pan de nuestro espíritu, y él llega a poseerlo será nuestra salvación y será nuestra alegría y regocijo del alma el que lo posee no temerá el enemigo que acecha en los rincones del camino de todo hombre por cuanto la vida es el producto del estudio y es equivalente con el conocimiento y la labor se nos hace un deber permanente y voluntario en nuestro primeros tiempos cuando aún tenemos a nuestro favor la juventud. Así que un hombre debe permanecer en actividad continua desde su juventud pues así es como la especie humana vino al mundo con la intención de aprender de la naturaleza y su evolución constante es por eso que también uno aprende de sí mismo pies también nosotros somos especiales junto con las demás especies del universo y nosotros debemos pues hacer nuestro convenio al nacer y cada día que pasa así estar de acuerdo con las leyes naturales del universo que nos han gobernado por miles de años y que más aun cuando llega el amanecer de un nuevo día se levantaría todos los días y poder sin duda vivir y compartir las casas que hay a disposición con un único motivo el de llegar a ser un admirador de la vida natural y así con la intención ver la realidad en su mente sin que uno diga que estaría solo y más bien en compañía con toda la naturaleza logrando un mutuo acuerdo de compartir todo con el otro y también llegar a ser un ser devoto a sus estudios y el vivir con los demás es para todos una grandiosa y alegre fiesta en donde todos participaríamos de las fiestas en cualquier momento, si se nos diera la oportunidad de llevar a los más ancianos el regalo de que es muy bienvenido en cualquier instante que así lo quisiera, y con nuestras manos nunca se verían vacías pues siempre sería un orgullo el visitar un hombre de sabiduría y riqueza espiritual que tanto bueno hace cuando por allí nos da la enseñanza cuando lo viese por lugares frecuentes por él. Y cuando aún el día no empieza en la calle de tierra se nos presentara con sus manos ocupadas con las herramientas del día para trabajar las tierra que lo ha visto crecer en el campo y haciendo las cosas que más guste con la gran alegría vio su productos en la calle de tierra y con más ganas de vivir en el pueblo donde nació para un día ser el que llevara sus productos al mercado y ofrecerlo al pueblo que le gusta tanto. Pero entre tanto que nos mantenemos en actividad y permanecemos activos durante el transcurso de la vida nos encontramos con muchos situaciones que debemos afrontar con nuestra propia y singular decisión pues aquí una vez más se nos prueba las facultades de la mente como un instrumento de aprendizaje y nuestra entendimiento nos alumbra la calle que uno debe seguir al transcurso de los años de vida y también nos da la oportunidad de hacernos grandes en inteligencia y también porque no los sentimientos del espíritu que llamamos de cariño y amor que más los necesitamos cuando uno se mira frente a frente con un personaje que nos llama la atención y nos indica el punto de vista de donde uno está presente en su interior y donde más que nuestro centro del corazón de donde el espíritu santo reside para así una vez más reestablecer una de las actividades del amor que como un fuego muy pasivo y abrazador nos hace tan amable la noche y por supuesto los días también, ya que es necesario para nuestra vida esta singular y delicada forma de convivir con el otro personaje de la vida en el planeta de los grandes y deliciosos frutos de amor, por eso cuando el sol sale en el oriente se nos da la oportunidad de abrazar el ser amado para que aquellos que se aman y se entregan con amor a la vida y nos nace del alma el sentimiento puro del amor se verán en felices y grandes fiestas de amor y aquí uno se pregunta que como sería la fiesta del amor cuando uno estuviera libre de toda falsa y corrupción espiritual y corporal que por allí pudiéramos recoger en el camino de la vida, sin propósito que hoy día abunda en el mundo; y desde allí por un hecho de conciencia despierta nosotros vemos el mundo tan triste y maltratado por la fuerza del mal que nos atrae hacia el hondo y oscuro abismo al que nosotros no más nos queda el sentimiento de lastima y horror el que sabe a azufre y el olor a muerte en donde las almas se purifican hasta que den señas de su amendamiento de los errores cometidos en la vida deliberadamente contra el personaje que uno tiene y tuviera que respetar y amar durante los días que vivimos en el mundo y sagrado lugar que se nos da la oportunidad de vivir en acordancia con nuestros sentimientos humanos

Hola a todos los amigos de pueblo a quienes yo hoy me dirijo con gran ilusión de prosperidad y también a los que hoy faltan por una u otra razón les haremos un cordial saludo con un minuto de silencio para recordar los tiempos de vida a lo que fue y será los grandes tiempos que vivimos juntos con los demás. Así que para esta temporada de verano ya pasada los amigos de pueblo se reunirán en los lugares más convenientes para felicitarse el uno al otro como lo han venido haciendo desde que todo el proyecto de seguir con las enseñanzas del pasado tan oscuro e incierto de los humanos por eso cuando alguno de nosotros falta es causa de mucho dolor espiritual pues para nosotros es como si fuésemos un alma o un espíritu viviendo en diferente cuerpo, es para todos nosotros un gran pesar también, entonces cuando el vendrá con su nuevo vestido de otro lado de la vida nos da un gran orgullo al ver sus vestiduras de completo honor y entre tanto la atmosfera se prepara para un gran festivo día que no podemos pasar desapercibido y por lo mismo no debemos de dejar los días pasar y que no se nos olvide la pena de nuestro hermano al salir de los grandes abismos de donde nosotros frecuentamos por muchos años en el pasado y con esta tan ocupada vida nos damos a celebrar los más ocultos procedimientos de bienvenida de los que un día en el pasado se alejaron de nosotros y dejando los recuerdos en la memoria de los que le querían para entonces el ya sería bienvenido y amado por todos. Y entonces para celebrar las fiestas de los que allí fueron caídos por las muerte que en cierta ocasión y en esta se vieran atrapados por los abismos de los mundos inferiores de la naturaleza un día cercano nos darán la sorpresa de llegar ante nosotros con la sonrisa del cielo y con gran entusiasmo volver a la vida con vestiduras del espíritu y el cuerpo renovado y sano para así ser una vez más los resurrecto del infierno en donde esperaron por tiempos de larga pena en donde aprendieron a mantener el estado y si duda de ser, pues eh ahí que a veces es duro afrontar el gran dolor y al paciencia sería muy fuerte para soportar la dura pena de la muerte en secreto y descender a los mundos inferiores en donde encontrarían los secretos de la vida y la muerte y al levantarse de donde estaba hallaría el mundo de los cielos tan frescos y puros como el roció de las mañanas en las rosas se le saturaran los con el olor de las floras del campo pues como ya hemos sabido que los hombres de bien se quedan en los lugares secretos y para más tarde venir por sorpresa al mundo de los cielos donde preservaran los tiempos de bien para y formando una vez mas parte de la familia del hombre una vez más y delante de los que así les hizo presa del tiempo y emancipación del movimiento pero para ahora todo será consumado y desvelado a la luz de la vida en donde moran por siglos y en la paz del señor les acogerán los tesoros del cielo y la pureza del roció sobre las floras en una mañana de invierno.

Para cuando llegaron las noticias de que un dia el mensajero llegara de lo alto de donde viene la sabiduria de los profetas y los que en los misterios del espiritu han estudiado y por supuesto aqui nos envian el mensaje del mundo de los ocultos y sagrados misterios de la creacion, en tanto que nos disponemos a tomar nuestras vidas para estudiar nuestro origen y destino pues son muchas las incognitas que podiamos asumir, y de caulquier manera seguir el camino de los que se dedican a estudiar la naturaleza y sus misterios que se encieran en el interior de la conciencia y origenes del despertar de nuestra vida, cuando empezo con la primera inalacion del aire y aparecimos en este mundo, para luego empezar nuestra existencia y viajar al mundo fisico para por primera vez poseer el precioso y pequeño cuerpo que es tan precioso, de tal manera uno va acumulando la fuerza para hacer las casas y mas adelante ser un individuo de positiva intencion para los fuuturos estudios del ser. En cuanto sea posible muchos son los que estudiamos los misterios de la vida y sus diversas escogencias que se nos ofrecen en el transcurso del nuevo amanecer y los pasos a seguir caundo sea un hombre capaz de decidir el camino a seguir y en un intento por sobrevivir en el mundo de que escogen el bien y el sacrificio por los demas en un intento por ser la familia de los que han de ser escogidos, y los que en Dios creyeron y confiaron sus destinos de ahora en adelante para seguir las enzeñansas de los profetas y la guia de los maestros de la sabiduria oculta en un intento por seguir el cause que nos llevara a la conquista de los tesoros de la vida intima y sus grandes atributos de los que un dia se dieron a la tarea de luchar contra los instintos de la parte negativa que en uno existen latentes para que cuando uno vea su supuesto intencion que es la de vivir en nuestro interior con el poposito de ser un ejemplo para la conciencia de nuestro ser, un gran espejo en donde uno se puede mirar y ver exacto el valor de nuestros actos y ser un campo de experimento y entrenamiento y superacion del gran y profundo misterio de la vida en si, y aqui en ese campo de superacion ser el triunfante de la si, un hombre de sabiduria y experiencia capaz de reconocerse en cualquier momento que asi lo quisiera, y entonces un humilde y poderoso ser que se levantara del profundo y oscuro sueño de donde proviene todo vida y que debemos alabar en todo momento que a nuestra memoria se presente ese primer pensamiento y el primer soplo de vida que inicio la vida del pequeño que con alegria nos recibieron los demas y enntonces vivir en el mundo de la luz y la conciencia en un lugar de mucha prosperidad y amor, entre tanto nosotros asi lo vamos a recibir cada dia sin el menor senitdo de duda y se nos presenta en nuestra vida en visiones en la mente y nustros ojos los testigos que cada dia nos da la luz de vida, la gran vision de los maestros y profetas del mundo que se dieron a la tarea de seguir los rayos del sol en la montaña fria y en la mañana se levantaron de sus lechos para ver la mañana nacer del tiempo el espacio se lleno de gran gran belleza con los primeros rayos del sol alla en lo alto de la montaña.